How to Build
Patios and
Decks

A Popular Science Book

How to Build
Patios and Decks

by Richard Day

Drawings by
Carl J. De Groote

POPULAR SCIENCE

HARPER & ROW
New York, Evanston, San Francisco, London

Times Mirror Magazines, Inc.
Book Division

Editor and Publisher	John W. Sill
Executive Editor	Henry Gross
Associate Editor	Neil Soderstrom
Art Director	Jeff Fitschen
Production Manager	Millicent La Roque
Editorial Assistant	Pat Blair

Library of Congress Catalog Card Number: 75-31065
ISBN: 0-06-011028-7
Cover photo courtesy of the California Redwood Association

Manufactured in the United States of America

I dedicate this book
to the weekend builder
who would like to add
outdoor living space
around his home.

ACKNOWLEDGMENTS

The author gratefully acknowledges the following firms for their help with this book: American Plywood Assn.; Brick Association of North Carolina; California Redwood Assn.; Cement and Concrete Assn. (England); General Electric Co.; Louisiana-Pacific Corp.; Miracle Adhesives Corp.; National Swimming Pool Inst.; and Western Wood Products Assn. He also thanks Edward D. Dionne and Franklin W. "Doc" Vaughan for their assistance in the preparation of this book.

Contents

1 | Planning the Patio or Deck

MANY OF THE PROBLEMS every homeowner experiences in planning or selecting his house are common to planning the deck or patio. These include recognizing the basic function of the new project, agreeing on style and design, selecting the proper site, meeting local building codes, grading and landscaping, providing for future expansion, and, of course, financing the project. But because many decks and patios are do-it-yourself projects, you'll experience the added benefits of pride of achievement plus great savings in labor and other costs by doing the hard but unskilled work yourself. You will dig trenches, haul supplies, buy materials at close-out sales.

The prospective patio/deck owner should be forewarned that there is no preconceived, packaged plan to fit all needs. Living styles vary and they change. Families shrink or grow. Thus, flexibility of design is the prime criterion of the most successful deck or patio.

Your desires for outdoor living may be met in the form of a standard deck or patio, a Florida room, a lanai, loggia, pavilion, or veranda. (See the Glossary of Outdoor Living at end of book.)

Spacious, although cozy . . . formal, yet relaxed . . . warmed by sunlight, but also cooled by gentle breezes . . . sheltered from rain and snow, but open to the changing wonders of nature—the patio/deck carries a big burden for any one area of a house. But, through proper planning, the answer to all these demands is available in a variety of forms.

Your earliest planning should include honestly appraising your own capabilities and limitations, and deciding what areas must be handled by a professional. If you use one, bring him into the project at the early stages, long before you make any working plans. His expertise should more than cover his fee. It's far easier to erase a pencil line from paper than to shore up a sagging deck or break up a crumbling wall because the footing did not extend below the frost line.

Your own local building department may be able to offer some advice free of charge. A good many offer printed typical designs that are acceptable in your area. Lumber yards quite often have qualified people who will check your plans without fee, provided that you buy the materials from them. Similarly, landscape architects who operate nurseries may offer their advice without charge, in return for the plantings order. In addition, your state university field service and county farm agent may offer information on soil control, frost lines, soil load limits, drainage problems—all without fee.

When planning a patio/deck, there's no better advice than that of Daniel Burnham: "Make no little plans." Although Burnham was a turn-of-the-century urban planner accustomed to thinking on a grand scale in laying out huge cities, his advice holds true today in planning a deck or patio. Small plans lack what it takes to fire your enthusiasm . . . or anyone else's.

1

SITE SELECTION. "Form follows function," said world-renowned architect Ludwig Mies van der Rohe. So the first step in planning is to define the project's function. Function includes such things as merely a quiet area for relaxation, as an informal outdoor family dining area, as a room for formal entertaining, as a hobby area for working on projects, or for growing flowers and vegetables the year around. A patio/deck can be a retreat for enjoying a view or for private sunbathing. It may be a coordinated family center overlooking the children's game area and swimming pool.

The well-planned deck or patio can ably serve all these functions at various times of the day and in changing seasons to suit varying moods of the family,

Once function is set, then comes site selection. The prime consideration in siting is solar orientation. That same *el sol* that creates a 115° summer day in Tucson offers little comfort in Duluth in December. But with good siting and adequate screening against wind and sun, the new addition can be enjoyed almost year-round.

Solar orientation simply means siting the patio/deck with attention to the constantly changing relationship between it and the sun. It's really not much of a problem when you keep in mind that the morning sun is relatively mild, but after 11 a.m. as it rises overhead and heads westward, solar heat can become intense — especially on an unshaded patio on the west or south side of the house. In summer, the north side of the house is coolest. In winter it can be bitterly cold.

Ideally, then, an outdoor living area is located on the east or north side of the house in summer, then is somehow shifted to the south or west side in winter. It's a neat trick if you can do it.

Making the best of site problems is one of the purposes of careful patio/deck planning. A sharply up-sloping lot is leveled with a Douglas fir deck backed by rock walls holding a terraced garden of evergreens. Ends of the 2 × 3 deck boards are cut to follow curve of the bank plantings.

Your planning may show that a series of small decks off several rooms can give more enjoyment than one larger deck of comparable area. A conversation corner of 2 × 4 Douglas fir planks set on edge over 4 × 6 treated fir beams expands the living room and offers a transitional step-down from house to exposed-aggregate concrete patio with treated fir dividers.

Western Wood Products Assn.

One answer is to build an L-shaped deck or patio, wrapping it around two sides of the house — north and west or east and south. Then you'll get both gentle morning sun and cool evening breezes.

Unfortunately, some building codes restrict the extension of decks and patios beyond the sides of a house, lest they intrude on a neighbor's privacy. But if your lot is big enough and there is no code objection, it's a fine way to cope with Old Man Sol.

Keep in mind these solar considerations:

East. The patio facing eastward will be cool after high noon, because it is shaded by the house. Such siting is excellent for a hot climate in summer. Adequate overheads and side enclosures or screening will take the chill from winter.

West. This is often the warmest area in summer so overhead or vertical screening is mandatory. It may even be necessary to set up portable electric fans in some areas that are subjected to intense sun during the summer. But in winter, any heat from the sun will be a delight. Overheads and screens should be adjustable, rather than of the permanent type, to control heat and glare all year around.

North. A north-exposed area is good only if totally enclosed, at least roofed over. The reason is that it seldom receives any sunlight, yet is subjected to rain and snow. Thus, it can in time become a musty, damp area, with the concrete overgrown with moss, the deck timbers mildewed, and the project not too suitable for raising flowers or relaxing in comfort. A comparatively inexpensive fiber-roofed glass enclosure with glassed wall panels can make this a highly enjoyable year-round area. Usually, supplemental cooling is not necessary, but portable electric space heaters can come in handy.

Sitting problem? This house had no space for a rear patio. The front yard was it — or nothing. The L-shaped house plan created a large, open rectangular area near the front entry, and this was made into a 20 by 30-foot concrete patio behind the shrubs and fence.

Privacy was obtained for the front patio by an attractive concrete-block-grille wall 5 feet high around two sides. The open grille-blocks let breezes through yet make interesting shadow patterns. Plantings soften the effect of the wall.

Patio with western exposure became unbearably warm for late afternoon and evening use. But its placement was required by traffic patterns, so a fiberglass-roofed metal-structured canopy was added for shade and shelter. To soften the sunlight, the patio was painted green to tie in with the adjoining grass.

Two-level western wood deck designed by Richard Miller affords an excellent traffic pattern with easy access to the kitchen. It eliminates the need for an outdoor grill. Upper platform is used for dining, lower for living. Easy-care plants, like yucca and mugho pines, make a delightful surrounding garden area.

Western Wood Products Assn.

The builder of a new home who contemplates a future patio or room enclosure is wise to have furnace ducts or heat pipes extended to that north wall when the house is built. Then, when a room is added, a heating vent is readily accessible by cutting through the outside wall.

South. In warm climates, this is the problem side of the house because it absorbs the sun's heat throughout the year. But in cooler climates, in winter, it's a delight to bask in warmth reflected off fresh snow. Overheads can readily control summer sun, but may have to be supplemented by curtains and screening. In northern climates, where snowfall is heavy, overheads should be strong enough to support a wet fall. One obvious answer is an open or egg-crate gridwork, covered with vines in the summer but that allows snow to fall through. Vertical screening will shut out the low sun in hot climates, and will serve as a windbreak for wintry conditions. Such screening may take the form of adjustable awnings, fences, or shrubbery. The vertical screens can be adjusted to operate from the bottom upwards in northern climes, thus keeping out wind but letting in sunlight.

The accompanying illustrations show how the problem of siting for solar orientation can be solved in a variety of ways.

Planning a house and patio from scratch provides the most opportunities for desirable results. It also illustrates how to attack the scale-model process with an existing house.

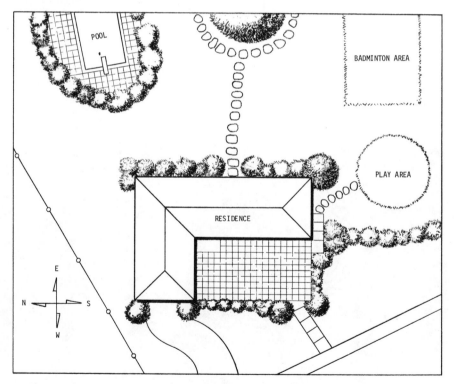

The patio here is at the front of the house and a screening wall built around it. Maximum wall height is governed by local regulations. Usually such walls may not stick out beyond the front line of the house.

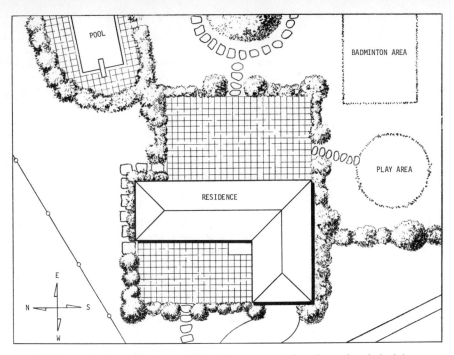

The house plan has been reversed—a trick you cannot do with an already-built house—to offer the west-facing patio some protection from the sun. This plan is more suited to a warm climate than a cold one.

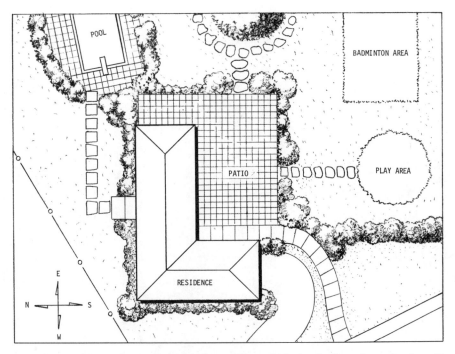

This plan is better for a cold climate. A south-facing deck absorbs the sun's rays in winter. The house itself screens the deck from north winds, yet the deck's L-shape permits following the sun throughout the day for warmth.

SCALING THE SITE PLAN. Second step in your planning is the drawing of a scaled plan of your lot. A scale of $\frac{1}{8}$ inch to the foot is usually convenient. Thus, if your lot is 80 by 100 feet, it will be reproduced on paper as an area 10 by $12\frac{1}{2}$ inches. The use of squared-off graph paper facilitates the plotting.

Begin by indicating the outer boundaries of your lot with heavy lines that will stand out. Then indicate the placement of your house within the lot lines. Only an outline form of the house need be drawn in, since you are not concerned with its interior.

Next indicate all permanent installations: driveways, sidewalks, underground sewer and gas lines, overhead or underground telephone lines, and easements, if any. These areas are taboo, and should not be interfered with. Similarly, a septic tank or its seepage field should be shown and avoided.

Then show with rough outlines all trees, hedges, shrubbery, and other greenery. Some may have to be transplanted. In other cases, the deck or patio will be built around trees. Fences are probably located along property lines, but these, too, should be indicated on the plan.

Finally, draw in all entrances to the house, any exterior electrical outlets (including light fixtures at the entrances), and outside garden-hose taps. Keep these utilities in mind for servicing your project. Property dimensions and those of the house may be drawn in for convenient reference. Then the scaled plan is complete.

What you are looking at, in effect, is a bird's-eye view of your property. It may be a busy sketch, but it will come in handy throughout construction. The more detailed you make it, the more useful it will be.

A deck designed to expand the living space of an older home makes good use of plants for screening and shade. Landscape designer Richard W. Painter provided a slot in the deck next to the house for the plantings.

Western Wood Products Assn.

Night lighting should be a consideration during the planning stage. A fixture close to the ground replaced a tall, glaring post lantern for a more esthetic appearance along a walkway. An opaque shield on top keeps light from shining into the eyes, directing it down onto the brick steps for safety.

Westinghouse Electric Co.

Now take a piece of shirt cardboard and cut out a rectangle or square of about the size to fit the patio or deck area you have selected. Although the final shape of the project need not be square or rectangular, this shape makes it easier to figure total square footage when materials are to be ordered.

Juggle the cardboard around in various positions in relation to the house. At first it may be too far east, or too far south. It may bump into trees, fences or a telephone pole. But eventually it will fit snugly into an unobstructed area. Do the same with other scaled pieces of cardboard and you'll discover possibilities for related decks or patios with paths to link them together.

When you are satisfied with the final siting on paper, you can go out and test your idea. You'll need a heavy hammer, some string, and at least four 2 × 2 wood stakes. Take these supplies to the site and pound one stake at each of the four proposed corners. Link them with a string-line to get a pretty good idea of what area of the yard the project will involve.

Check closely for anything you may have missed on the plan, such as overhead wires or dead branches. Also check: shrubs that need transplanting; access to outside water taps; traffic pattern to and from the house — especially to the kitchen; stairwells to the basement; steps rising overhead. Will your favorite view be obstructed if a solid wall is added to enclose the deck or patio? If so, better plan on glass windows. If not, a storage area may be added to hold yard or patio equipment used only when entertaining. Will the plot interfere with your own privacy, or that of your neighbors?

If all these things work out, then measure the area within the chalkline as a double-check against your scaled drawing. This gives the square footage or top surface area. As a rule of thumb, it should be about 20 percent of the house floorspace. Perhaps more, but hardly less.

Your scaling work is only half done at this stage. Too often the homeowner is disappointed with his new creation when he puts furniture on it and realizes that it's a bit too small. One basic (but usually unforeseen) reason is that decks and patios by their nature invite spacious living, more so than any interior room. A person likes to

An up-to-date Douglas fir deck was part of remodeling a gracious old colonial-style home. The larger deck was built at floor level for fuller access to the house. Built-in benches provide plenty of seating while taking up little space. Architects for this project were Fletcher & Finch.

stretch out and unwind when he arrives home. The too-small deck or patio defeats this purpose. A second reason is that outdoor furniture is larger than the interior stuff and occupies more floor area. Built-in furniture along the exterior walls will help by taking up less space. The only way to plan enough space is through a scale plan of the patio or deck itself. For this, a scale of ½ inch to the foot is more suitable than the earlier ⅛-inch scale used for the entire lot. Thus, a patio designed to be 20 feet square would be drawn 10 inches square, with the furniture also scaled ½ inch to the foot.

Then create the scale cutouts of furniture and equipment you intend to use there — things like picnic table and benches, deck chairs, serving table, perhaps a television set, barbecue, hobby equipment. The list depends on your own interests and the function of the facility.

In placing scaled furniture cutouts on the plan, be sure to allow enough space around them. This is activity area. You and your family will usually be carrying items and moving around more than in a formal living room. Provide clear traffic patterns both to the house entrance and access to any exterior electrical outlets that might be added. Keep in mind, too, that outdoor furniture may have to be stored in the winter, so there should be storage facilities nearby. Such areas may be located under built-in benches around the perimeter of the project.

When you are satisfied with your furniture plan, your scaling work is over. But if the area is too small, then your only recourse is to stretch at least one of the sides to accommodate all your needs. A foot or two can usually be gained by adjusting the stakes and stringline. And remember, you needn't think in terms of squares and rectangles; free-form patios and decks are usually casual and more relaxing to be in. Curvilinear forms are always graceful, but a circle of 20 feet diameter offers lots less area than a square measuring 20 feet on each side. It's geometry!

You are now ready to discuss your project with local building officials. They'll make sure you are not violating any codes, and will tell you whether a building permit is required. This may not seem so, but it's an important point affecting your property taxes for years to come. Generally, a building permit is required for either a patio or a deck. However, if it isn't, don't get one because the permit alerts the assessor that you've improved your property. You'd just as soon he didn't find out and raise your property valuation. This bit of advice was passed on by an assessor himself.

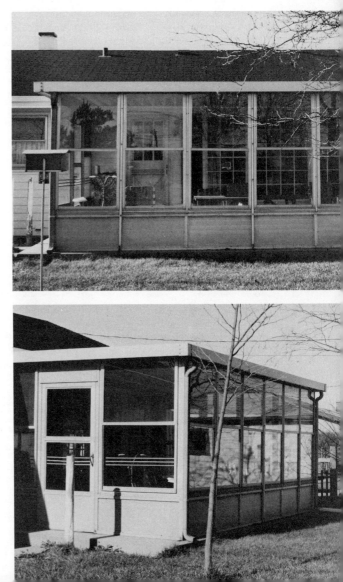

If the only decent location you have for a patio or deck is on the north side of the house in a cold climate, you can screen it in. This project was done on the pay-as-you-go plan. First, the 12 by 20-foot concrete patio was built. Two years later, a corrugated aluminum roof with integral gutter system went over it. In the third stage two years later, triple-track combination aluminum storm window-screen units and doors were added. These permit full use of the room, summer and winter. Electricity is carried through the house wall to the enclosed patio. Push-bars inside the aluminum doors and side windows are to protect children from contact with the glass; otherwise safety glass would be called for.

MEETING CODES. Often a homeowner decides he can build a patio or deck in a few days of vacation without bothering to touch bases with the local building department. "Once it's built," he reasons, "they can't make me tear it down."

Quite often he later learns, "Yes they can!"

Building codes are local standards for the construction of a building or improvement to a house. Zoning ordinances pertain to structural setbacks, structure heights, fence heights and styles, the vague area of esthetics, and similar factors relating to the effect of the project on the neighborhood. The intent of such restrictions is basically sound: to assure the property owner and his neighbors—the community as a whole—

Application for Building Permit

VILLAGE OF OLYMPIA FIELDS, ILLINOIS

Application Filed .... 19 ... Permit Issued .... 19 ...

Application is hereby made for a permit for: ☐ proposed building or ☐ alteration.

Class of building: Residence ...... Commercial ......

Sign Board ...... Other ......

Temporary structure ......

To be erected on lot No. ...... Block ......

Sub-Division ......

VOLUME NO.				ITEM NO.			
SEC.	TOWN	RANGE	LOT	SUB LOT	LOT	BLOCK	
PERMANENT NO.							
COPY FROM LAST TAX BILL							

Street and Number ......

Owner's Name ...... Phone ......

Address ......

Architect ...... Phone ......

Address ......

General Contractor ...... Phone ......

Address ...... Village License No. ......

Electrical Contractor ...... Phone ......

Address ...... Village License No. ......

Plumbing Contractor ...... Phone ......

Address ...... Village License No. ......

Surveyor ...... Phone ......

Address ......

Water Supply: Public Supply ☐ Private Well ☐ Well Driller ......

Sewer: Public Sewer ☐ Seepage System ☐ Results of percolation tests ......

Refrigeration or air conditioning: Yes ☐ No ☐ Horsepower ......

Will excavation under public street or walk be necessary? Yes ☐ No ☐

Will construction access be across public sidewalk or parkway? Yes ☐ No ☐

Will materials be stored on street, parkway, or sidewalks? Yes ☐ No ☐

Area of building in square feet, less porch, garage, breezeways and other open areas ......

TOTAL COST OF BUILDING

This application shall be accompanied by three sets of plans, three sets of specifications, also survey plat in triplicate of the premises showing legal boundary lines; easements, building set back lines and all public utilities; structures on adjoining lots; wells, septic tank and drainage field on adjoining lots; grades at wall of adjoining buildings, street, sidewalk and at intervals on property; together with application fee.

Affidavit made by Architect or Engineer of project showing true estimated cost of project, and state that to the best of his knowledge and belief the plans and specifications comply with the Village of Olympia Fields Building Code.

The applicant hereby certifies to the correctness of the above and agrees to construct the above building in strict compliance with all provisions of the Zoning Ordinance and the Building Regulations of the Village Code, and amendments thereto.

Approved for Permit:

.... Signature ....

Building Commissioner Owner or Approved Agent

DATE .... 19 ... Address ......

of good construction based on accepted designs. Unfortunately, many building codes are archaic and unnecessarily restrictive. Advances in construction, machinery, and materials make them so. Consequently, the trend has been to avoid such outdated or no longer pertinent codes in an effort to get the job done quickly and to save money. But a by-the-book building inspector who is a stickler for codes he helped draft can raise problems. It's safest to work with, not against, your building officials.

The accompanying illustration shows a typical application for a building permit. Many of the questions may not apply to your area, but the form serves as a checklist of what may be required.

	FEE	RESERVE	PAID	DATE	CHECK #	TO WHOM PAID
APPLICATION	$					
Construction Permit Sq. ft. of - Livable Area _____ Non-livable Area _____	$					
Electrical Permit No. of rooms _____	$					
Plumbing Permit No. of outlets _____ and inspection points	$					
Water tap - Long ☐ Short ☐	$					
Heating Permit	$					
Refrigeration Permit H/P of Unit _____	$					
Public Works Permit	$					
Well Permit	$					
Foundation Permit	$					
Sewer Connection Fee	$					
Septic Sewage Permit	$					
Sign Permit	$					
TOTAL	$					

DEPOSIT AND/OR SURETY BONDS		DATE POSTED	COMPANY	DISPOSITION
Contractor's Surety	$1,000.00 Bond			
Contractor's Deposit	$			
Excavation Under Public Street or Sidewalk	$			
Plumber's Surety	$500.00 Bond			

Typical building-permit application shows the kind of information required to get permission to construct a patio or deck.

THE MONEY TREE. If you're not independently wealthy and don't know anyone who is, getting your hands on enough cash these days to build a sizable patio or deck can be a major difficulty. Approach this problem with a lot of cool and you'll get further.

First of all, why not save up and pay cash? Can you wait? If not, how about making a cautious start and quitting when the money runs low? Start again when you're flush. Pay-as-you-go is by far the most satisfying method of construction. The lowest-cost, too.

Can't pay, and can't wait? Then you'll have to borrow. If you're willing to pay interest—the cost of using someone else's hard-saved money—this may not be too bad. It gets your project off the ground quickly. The best way to borrow is to pay the lowest interest rate available to you and to repay in the shortest possible time. This keeps down the cost of borrowing. Generally the lowest borrowing rates are found on a whole- or straight-life insurance policy that has been around long enough to have built up a decent cash value. You can borrow up to the amount of the cash value of the insurance policy. Payback can be as you feel it. No one hounds you. However, you keep right on paying the interest every year on the entire amount not paid back.

Another insider's place to borrow is at a credit union, if you belong to one. Rates tend to be lower than you'd get elsewhere. The payback terms can be arranged to suit, within the stricter limitations of the credit union.

Next in line is a bank loan. Go to the place where you bank and ask about one. A number of banks have home-improvement loan plans ready-made for customers. The project serves as security for the loan. If your credit is good enough, the banker may even make you an unsecured loan on just your signature. Then you needn't show plans for the project. Also, it won't be legally attached if you fail to pay on time. Some savings and loan firms have similar home-improvement loan plans.

Part of planning is making sure there are outdoor electrical outlets where you need them. Modern, sensible electrical codes now require that all these outlets be protected by ground-fault circuit interrupters (GFI's), as well as use weatherproof hardware, here by General Electric. These fail-safe shock protectors will add about $40 to your cost.

In your planning, be sure to allow enough room for the extra-large size of most outdoor furnishings. They stretch out like you'll want to on your patio and take up more space than indoor counterparts.

Western Wood Products Assn.

If you owe much less on your home mortgage than the house is worth, you can refinance the house with a new mortgage that pays off the old one, and gives you enough cash to pay for your project. Watch it, though, because if the new mortgage goes at a higher rate, the cost to convert could be astronomical over the years. Also, home mortgages get you involved in things like closing costs and other fees you'd best avoid. It's not the recommended way of financing a home improvement.

Some older home mortgages feature an open-end provision that lets you add onto them when you want money for such as a new patio. Check this out. It's a good way of getting money when you don't have it.

The Federal Housing Administration has a whole series of home-improvement loans at special low FHA-insured rates. The actual money, however, comes from a local lender, and so you may find him unwilling to suffer the red tape involved in getting your insured loan. He may convince you that his own plan is the better way to go. It may well be.

If you don't mind paying higher rates of interest, you can buy the materials for your project on credit and pay back by the month, plus interest. Sears and Wards have such plans, spelled out in their catalogs. If you contract out the work, contractors can help you to arrange easy financing.

The costliest place of all to borrow is from a finance company. Most charge the maximum allowable interest rates, well above bank rates. But if your credit isn't established at a bank, this method may still be open.

No matter where you borrow to build, the lender is required by law to give you a full-disclosure statement showing the true annual-interest rate of the unpaid balance and other facts like the amount of monthly payments and time to pay up.

One advantage of borrowing to build is that you enjoy the project now, not later. Payback, you'll find, gets easier as the months go by, because you're doing it with inflated dollars. But that's why the interest rates are so high in the first place.

2 | Ideas You Can Use

IDEAS ARE CHEAP. It's the working-out that makes them worthwhile. Here are a bunch of ideas worked out by others. There are no patents. You're free to use them as you like, intact or changed.

A great deal can be done with a few good ideas if you know how to bend them to your wishes, even when you don't know exactly what your wishes are. Take any patio or deck you see or any feature of one. Run it through the idea mill one by one, letting your mind create. Some of what you dream up may be just what you're looking for. And that's your *own* idea.

It works like this: You see a neighbor's wood deck with an edging of flowers. You like it, but don't want to be a copier. Apply the idea-mill specifics to it. Start with *smaller*. How would it look half the size? Three-fourths? Or take *larger*. How would it be half again as big? How about *unbordered*? What would elimination of the flowerbed edging do to it? Or bordered with large plantings instead of the small flowers the neighbors used?

Take *narrower*? How would it look made with narrower 2 × 4 planks set on edge instead of the wide decking your neighbor used? Try *changed order*. Suppose the flowers were planted between the deck and house instead of as a border? How would that go? Could the deck be made of alternating wide and narrow planks for a change of order?

How about *split up*? What if you built the deck as two or three separate ones instead of the one large one? Or *put together*? Suppose you incorporated the flower edging into the deck instead of using it as a border?

Get the idea? It works with any creation, whether you start with a borrowed idea or work on an idea of your own to improve it. Chances are, every successful product, method, or design went through an idea mill, either consciously or subconsciously, before it hit the streets.

If you'll take your starter idea through the whole list, spending perhaps a minute on each item thinking, you can't tell what fascinating new design you'll create. When you finally build it, invite the neighbors over. See if they don't remark, "What a beautiful deck! Where did you ever get the idea?" Don't tell them.

By studying the accompanying photos and looking at decks and patios created by others, you'll find your first thoughts giving way to more sophisticated schemes. For instance, early on, you may have limited your project's concept to a simple, rectangular shape. Now, instead of straight lines and 90° angles, envision the project as being free-form, with flowing curves creating a kidney shape or a large circular area.

Or try these ideas:

- Leave a 3-foot-diameter hole at one corner to serve as a barbecue pit.
- Don't cut down that majestic tree that's standing exactly where you'd like the patio located. Instead, build around it, keeping pavement well back from the tree

base to allow for air and water to the roots. Or use brick or flagstone set in sand around the tree. Later, if you wish, you can roof over the project, building the new roof close to the upper tree trunk and filling in the intervening gap with foam rubber. Any rain seepage will trickle down the tree trunk, thus watering the roots – a job you'll have to supplement with a garden hose.

- Put your concrete patio to double duty by incorporating a shuffleboard court or children's play area.
- Add a 4-inch raised lip around the patio slab to serve as a retaining wall for water in the winter, thus creating an ice-skating rink, climate permitting.
- Where the ground slopes steeply, or is constantly wet, either create a raised deck or build a retaining wall and fill in the area with soil, thus creating a terrace that can be paved.
- Avoid purchasing chairs and other outdoor furniture by creating built-in seating along the edges of the deck or patio. Such integral furniture is always a space saver and is especially inviting when outdoor-type cushions are added.

Southern Pine Assn.

Steps built into a multilevel Southern-pine deck keynote an add-on that goes with the house's rough-sawn Southern-pine siding. Kick-out (foreground) can hold a large planter.

Rooftop deck made of Douglas fir 2 × 4's gains considerable design impact from a storage/privacy wall at one end. Roof trellis and potted plants add a lot, too. Deck sections are made to lift off for maintenance of the garage roof below. Architects are Farnham & Peck.

Easily made brick patio is surrounded by massive seat-height walls that incorporate a brick barbecue. Floor and access walks are bricks set in mortar on concrete slabs.

Masonite's Vacation Cabin extends the indoors with a spacious wood deck outside the living room. Open roof above the deck adds light.

Easy-care grass-level concrete patio measuring 25 feet on a side connects with the rear door by a short concrete walk. The diamond pattern was scored into the fresh concrete surface with a jointing tool and the pattern dusted on with concrete coloring. When the coloring faded, the owner painted over it.

General Electric Co.

Create a small but secluded living area away from the house by attaching a reflector lamp to an umbrella pole and aiming it upwards into the umbrella. A canopy of reflected light results. Surrounding foliage is accented by outdoor floodlights.

Two sizes of exposed-aggregate concrete tiles were set on the ground, surrounded by gravel, and wood-edged to form a textured patio leading from the house door. Edging lumber must be pressure-treated or made of rot-resistant wood.

Deck living at its finest on a broad L-shaped porch deck places the people in the space between house and garden. Designer Alexander Diepenbrock made the deck jog around planting beds. Shin-high fir railings at the corners make picture frames for gnarled oak trees.

Western Wood Products Assn.

Western Wood Products Assn.

Slight level changes in wood decks should present no problem. Simply build on steps (center) or pads (left) of the same material. Railings, too, can be an integral part of the deck.

You'll find lots to borrow in this idea-filled deck. Beams of the upper deck extend beyond the edge, both for structural appearance and to provide firm attachment for the doubled posts that support the unusual, attractive railing. Beam ends are chamfered for a finished look. Level change is accomplished with simple wood steps made in the conventional manner by notching 4 × 12 timbers. Lower level is only a step down to a loose-laid brick walk.

Western Wood Products Assn.

Live in a mobile home? No need to forego the beauties of a patio/deck. Build whatever you like within your lot restrictions. A well designed one features a slatted wood overhead for sun protection, plus an on-ground wood deck and matching fencing for privacy. Note how add-on roof pads keep rain off the entries. Fence grillework design at entrance is easy to make, airy yet private.

This circular concrete patio by architect Paul Courtland is divided into no-crack sections by redwood 2 × 4s. Low redwood retaining wall around one-third of the patio is made from 2 × 12s doubled and set on end in the ground. Part of the wall is topped with a striking redwood seat made of spaced 2 × 6s. Heart redwood, though not cheap, does not rot, making it ideal for outdoor use.

California Redwood Assn.

Got a view? Make the most of it by locating your patio/deck to look out on it. While some privacy is sacrificed, the results can be worth it. Multilevel exposed-aggregate concrete patio was formed with leave-in redwood 2 × 4s and 2 × 6s. The inviting redwood bench at left is attached to posts in the ground.

California Redwood Assn.

EFFORT INVOLVED. During the idea-mill stages, try to let your mind go; don't restrain it. List all ideas you get along the way. They call this brainstorming. It works just as well with more than one person. The only rule is: no negative thinking. No criticism. No "but that's never been done before." Not at this point. Negative thinking puts a damper on successful brainstorming. Just assume that anything can be done and that all ideas as conceived are excellent ones.

At some point after the ideas have been collected and recorded, get down to critical thinking, which is quite different from creative thinking. For one thing, it's much easier. There are critics everywhere, but few creators. During the critique, your ideas can be tempered with the practical. Can they be made to work? How? How much would they cost? Can you do the work yourself? Where will the materials come from? If it has never been done before, can you do it? Can you afford it? Do you have the time? Is it too much for your house? Will it really make the kind of patio/deck you want?

Temper your creative thinking to the point where you won't be in over your head for money, time, work, skills, or space. Plan big but not overboard. Don't forget, though, that big plans can be taken on, one small step at a time, yet still be big plans with all their psychological charisma.

Remember, too, that you needn't change ideas in order to use them. Anything that you see in this book can be stolen outright, if you like. While some of the idea originators might object to commercial use of their creations, no one will mind if you use an idea yourself at home.

Also, consider going to a professional for ideas. While this may not be the cheapest approach, it can easily turn out to be the most pleasing one, as many of these photos will attest.

3 | Tools for Building

PART OF THE MONEY YOU SAVE by building your own deck/patio may well be invested in getting the right tools for the job. Chances are, you already have some of them, perhaps even a good many. The basic tools, at least: hammer, tape measure or rule, saw, pencil (it's a tool, too), square, screwdriver. But you may be lacking some of the more specialized tools such as sledge hammer, tube level, cement-mason's jointing tool.

The exact tools you need will depend on what kind of patio or deck you're planning to build. Building a wood deck calls for woodworking tools. Building a concrete slab calls for cement-finishing tools. They're not interchangeable.

In any case, it is almost certain that you will have to buy some tools. You'll want to rent costly tools that likely will be used only once.

In half a lifetime of writing articles and books on do-it-yourself home-handyman subjects, I've developed a philosophy on tools that you may find helpful, especially if you have lots of tools yet to acquire. Manufacturers sometimes send me their new tools to try out and appraise for possible publicity. In this way I get to test far more tools than when I was an interested do-it-yourselfer. Along the way I learned that quality tools may cost more (I don't get 'em all given to me), but they are *always* worth the difference.

At first glance you may not find much difference between a hammer chosen from the "any-tool-99-cents" bargain bin at your dealer's and a Stanley Steelmaster hammer, say. They both pound nails. But it's *how* they pound nails that counts. And also *how long* they'll go on pounding nails, though that is lesser because you can buy lots of 99-cent hammers for the higher cost of a Stanley Steelmaster. The better tool is better balanced, better designed for driving nails. You soon find that you bend over far fewer nails with the better hammer. This brings you satisfaction. The better hammer is more comfortable to use, too. You soon feel as though it's an extension of your hand. It is safer, also. The heat-treated steel face is less likely to chunk off and possibly hit someone in the eye.

When it comes to pulling nails, there is no comparison between a quality hammer and a cheapie. The better hammer has wedge-shaped claws designed to grip even headless nails and pull them. An economy hammer does not.

If you've ever held a house-raising party with a bunch of helpful neighbors over to build walls and erect them, you know how quickly your best hammers get grabbed up by even the less-experienced workers. They can feel the difference, too. "This is *my* hammer," they'll say defensively when you need one for yourself. "Go get one of your own."

GET THE BEST. The same is true of saws, chisels, trowels, measures, every tool. There is a difference, one that shows up when you use the tool. So my advice is to

Some of the basic tools you'll need are (from top): claw hammer, 8-point crosscut handsaw, tape measure, pencil, chalk line, carpenter's square (a try-square will do), and 2-foot-long level. You may already have many of these tools.

spend a little more and get the best tool. Then plan to take care of it properly and use it for a lifetime. Avoid the bargain bins and buy brand names that you know.

And even buy the best models among those. For instance, Stanley makes several hammers from good to outstanding. The prices will tell you which is which. Buy the highest-priced one.

I admit there may be another side to it: buy cheap, replace often, and always have new-looking tools. I'm just giving you my side: buy the very best tools you can afford.

As with most competing products, if you shop around enough, you'll find several top brands of each type of tool. It probably matters little which of those you select. All are excellent. Through experience, though, I've developed some favorites that, on risk of making a few enemies, I'll pass along to you.

For hand tools I like Stanley, as you may have already guessed. A good many professionals also feel this way, so I'm in good company. Disston, as well as Stanley, makes really good hand saws. Cement-finishing tools by Marshalltown can be counted on for quality. In power tools I've found none better than Black & Decker. Compared with others, they *look* well made. Some, like B&D drills, are priced unbelievably low. Both Sears' and Wards' top lines of hand and power tools are good, in my experience. And you can't beat their availability.

Before tackling a patio or deck project, look over the lists of tools you'll need and compare them with those you already have. This will give you a rough idea of which tools you are in the market for, and you can start shopping for them ahead of time. It beats running out to find a float while a concrete patio is fast setting.

If you do any electrical wiring or plumbing along with your project, or put a roof over your deck, you may need other specialized tools for doing those jobs.

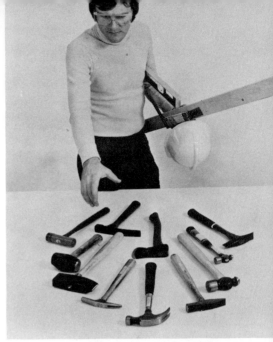

If your tools are patched-up and worn out like the hammer (foreground), toss them away and get new ones. The Hand Tools Institute says hammers with broken handles, split faces, and loose heads can be dangerous.

Which hammer should you use? The one that fits the job. Hammers shown are designed for such jobs as nailing wood, nailing and drilling masonry, splitting masonry units, striking chisels, tacking, chipping mortar, riveting, splitting wood, driving stakes, etc. Use the wrong one and you may chip the heads.

Concrete-finishing tools that you may want for building a concrete patio, are (top to bottom): sponge-rubber float for making a textured finish; edging tool for rounded edges; steel trowel for a smooth finish; magnesium float for a non-slip finish; and wood float for the initial floating required on all jobs.

Hammer construction makes a difference in the way the tool works. Stanley Fiberglass hammer has a specially tempered head that is taper-bonded to the fiberglass-reinforced plastic handle for strength in hammering and nail-pulling. Cushioned rubber handle gives a comfortable, strong grip.

If your project is too far from an electrical outlet to connect an ordinary electric drill, a cordless model will save work in drilling for pilot holes and deck attachments.

A router is a handy tool for putting an attractive edge on deck railings, posts, trim. You can get a variety of bits that let you rout different patterns in wood.

TOOLS YOU'LL PROBABLY NEED

Basic Tools
Pencil
Tape measure
Yard-long metal rule
Chalk line and chalk
Try-square
Level, 2'
Wood chisel, ¾"
Hand drill and bits
Hammer, 13-16 oz.
Hand saw, 8-point
Screwdriver, 10"
Plumb bob
Sledge hammer, 5-10 lb.
Paint brush

Earth-Handling Tools
Shovel, long-handled
Spade, 4" wide
Post-hole digger
Tamper (home-built)
Garden rake
Wheelbarrow, garden-type

Useful Portable Power Tools
Jig saw or saber saw
Electric drill, ¼" or ⅜"
Circular saw
Sander, belt or orbital
Chain saw, 10"-12" guide bar
Router
Table or radial saw
Paint sprayer
Extension cord, No. 16, 25'-50'

Rental Tools
Concrete mixer
Power compacter

Electric drill, ½"
Concrete chute
Contractor's wheelbarrow
Tractor with blade
Concrete pumping service

Concrete Tools
Strikeboard (long, straight 2 × 4)
Darby, 3½" by 4', or bull float, 8" by 4'
Wood float, 4" by 15"
Steel trowel, 4" by 16"
Jointing tool, 1" bit
Edger
Hoe
Mason's line
Wire brush
Garden hose
Pails
Brooms
Knee-boards

Other Useful Tools
Tube level
Stanley Surform shaver
Plane, 8" or 10"
High-speed wood bits, ⅜" to 1"
Plastic-faced hammer (for wood chisel)
Clamps, large, adjustable
Magnesium float
Sponge-rubber float
Hacksaw
Sawhorses (2)
Plastic curing sheet
Carpenter's square
Line level
Spiral push-pull screwdriver
Trigger hose nozzle
Crowbar

Much handwork is saved with a portable circular saw. Fitted with a combination saw blade, it can crosscut and rip boards in a fraction of the time it takes by hand. Little electric power is used. Black & Decker's Sawcat, shown, features a sawdust-ejection system that keeps the cutting line clear.

A tube level is not an absolute necessity, but darned useful to have. Sure-Level is by Schuyler Products Inc., Kingston, N.Y. It costs little, and attaches to the ends of any ½" hose. Filled with water, and with air bubbles eliminated, it transfers levels accurately across long distances, as when you're leveling for a deck.

Crowbar with a new twist, this new one is called "Sweetie-Pry," by its manufacturer, J. D. F. Enterprises, Placentia, Calif. Its right-angle handle fits in where ordinary crowbars cannot, making it more useful. Available in lengths of 17, 27, and 37 inches.

If you are serious about woodworking, and planning to build a wood deck, there's no better time to get a radial saw than before you start. It crosscuts, rips, cuts at angles, ploughs, dadoes, grooves, and does almost whatever you want to shape and size lumber. Cuts are made on top of the board where you can see them.

Surform shaver by Stanley Tools does a job similar to that of a wood rasp, but works faster and cleaner. The perforated blade is replaceable once it finally dulls. Use a Surform for rounding off corners, shaping wood to fit. Many styles are available.

Magnetic carpenter's level by Stanley contains a magnet-impregnated plastic strip along one edge that lets it cling to an iron or steel surface while you're accurately leveling, plumbing, or adjusting to a 45° slope.

Shortie level, also magnetic, is handy for quick leveling where length and great accuracy don't count, such as when installing deck planking or leveling pier tops.

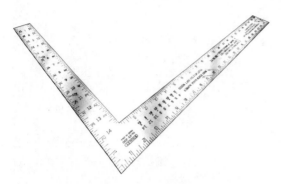

A carpenter's square is not a "must" tool for patio/deck building, but one can come in handy, especially for cutting stair stringers. This aluminum one is imprinted with lots of useful information, such as a metric conversion table.

Stanley Tools

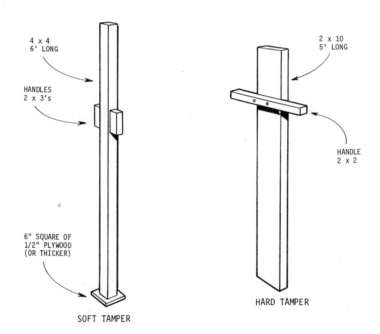

4 x 4
6' LONG

HANDLES
2 x 3's

6" SQUARE OF
1/2" PLYWOOD
(OR THICKER)

SOFT TAMPER

2 x 10
5' LONG

HANDLE
2 x 2

HARD TAMPER

HOME-BUILT TAMPERS

Some tools are too costly for a patio or deck-building project. If you need a small tractor for pushing dirt or leveling or backfilling, you can rent it by the hour. This unit has a front bucket plus a rear backhoe, both hydraulically powered.

Plan to get good tools and take care of them for a lifetime of use. Waxing the metal parts after a project will keep them from rusting until you're ready to use them again. Ordinary past wax does the job without hurting tool performance. It actually helps the saw next time out.

4 | Building a Wood Deck

THE BIGGEST, LOWEST-COST ROOM you can add to your house is a deck. That, plus a privacy screen or sun shade sets your family up for great outdoor living. Outdoor dining, entertaining, sunning, or just relaxing all are activities suited to a deck. What's more, working with wood is a pleasant pastime.

Wood decks fit in anywhere. They can be laid on the ground—using specially treated rot-resistant wood—or held up in the air on posts of practically any length. They're suited to level areas as well as steeply sloping ones. A deck can be built over an old roof, such as above the garage. Or it can extend from a second story. A deck need be no more than a step up off the ground.

Decks can be low-level, high-level, hillside, or rooftop, depending on where they're built. All except the rooftop ones are usually planked with spaced wood boards that drain quickly after a rain. A rooftop deck is usually covered with exterior-type plywood that may be joint-caulked with an elastomeric sealant and even waterproofed.

A low-level deck is supported either on the ground or on piers and posts very short and close together. A well-drained location is vital to maintaining soil support for such a deck. Decks laid on the ground are usually placed on a 3-inch layer of gravel for best drainage. All wood within six inches of the ground should be pressure-treated or rot-resistant to prevent decay (check your code on this; some codes require a greater distance).

A high-level deck is usually supported on 4 × 4 posts. The portion that is attached to the house is often supported by it. This support must be firmly fastened to house framing, not merely to the siding (see drawing).

Hillside decks are used to create usable outdoor living space on steep slopes. While they cost more than a level yard, they still cost lots less than equal indoor space. Support is the same as for a high-level deck—use heavy beams between posts. Posts are spaced far apart for a less busy appearance underneath, and for economy of materials. (More on that coming up.)

You can make use of a rooftop deck only if your roof was originally designed as a floor. That means roof loading is equivalent to the heavier floor loading required by most codes. Most roofs aren't. Your building official can tell you.

ABOUT LUMBER. Before you can design a deck, you'll want to know several things about the wood selected to build it. Wood, as you know, comes from trees. And trees are almost as individual as people: some strong, some weak; some hard, some soft. Each species of wood—redwood, pine, fir, and such—differs from another in many characteristics. So does each board cut from the same tree. Some contain knots, sap streaks, twisted grain and other defects that make them vary in strength. These variances are covered by lumber grading. As each board comes from the lumber

Wood deck of long-span 2 × 3s set on edge graces an entrance. Bench and planter of the same wood repeat the theme. Setting planks on edge puts the wood up where you can see it, minimizes under-deck structure.

Cantilevered deck juts out from the house below, supported on beams held by angled braces cut into the framing. Complicated designs like this call for professional advice.

mill's big saw, a lumber expert decides how good a board it is and stamps it with a grade mark. These differ as school grading systems but, for dimension lumber like that you'll be using to build a deck, grade marks are standard in the United States and Canada. The light-framing grades (2 to 4 inches wide and thick) are Construction, Standard, and Utility, in descending order. The joist and plank grades (2 to 4 inches thick, 6 inches and wider) are Select Structural (really nice!), No. 1, No. 2, and No. 3. Neither Utility nor No. 3 should be used to build a deck. They're poor looking and acting grades.

Most decks are built of Douglas fir, Southern pine, or redwood. All are easy-working woods that have excellent strength (fir and Southern pine much more so than redwood). Construction heart-variety redwood has the added advantage of being free from rot even when in contact with the ground. No finish is ever needed on it, making it fine for decking. On the other hand, redwood is becoming quite costly and may even be unavailable at times. Recommended are the lower-cost "Garden Grades" of redwood (see your lumber dealer).

Other species that are suitable for deck-building include ash (tough and hard to work but strong), Western red cedar (easy-working and rotproof but not very strong),

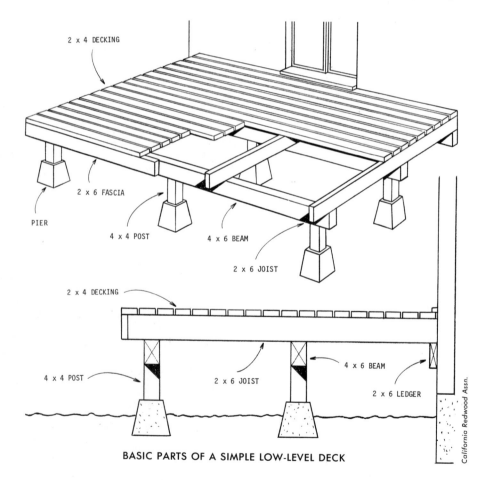

BASIC PARTS OF A SIMPLE LOW-LEVEL DECK

California Redwood Assn.

cypress (rotproof), larch (similar to Douglas fir), gum, hemlock, white fir, soft pines, poplar, and spruce.

The best wood for beams is Douglas fir, ash, or Southern pine because of their strength. The best decking woods are Douglas fir, Southern pine, redwood, cedar, Western larch, and cypress because of their decay-resistance, stiffness, strength, wear-resistance, and freedom from warping.

Lumber sizes are always given as nominal. The real sizes (in inches) are:

Nominal	Actual
1″	3/4″
2″	1$\frac{1}{2}$″
4″	3$\frac{1}{2}$″
6″	5$\frac{1}{2}$″
8″	7$\frac{1}{4}$″
10″	9$\frac{1}{4}$″
12″	11$\frac{1}{4}$″

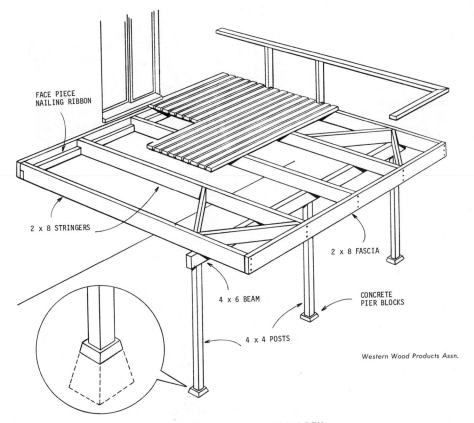

FACE PIECE
NAILING RIBBON

2 x 8 STRINGERS

2 x 8 FASCIA

CONCRETE
PIER BLOCKS

4 x 6 BEAM

4 x 4 POSTS

Western Wood Products Assn.

CONSTRUCTION OF RAISED DECK

A 2 × 4, thus, actually measures 1½ by 3½ inches when dry. "Green," un-seasoned lumber measures slightly larger, a 2 × 4 scaling $1\frac{9}{16}$ by $3\frac{9}{16}$ inches. Don't use green lumber because it shrinks too much.

Plywood, as might be used for a solid deck, is graded by different standards because it is a manufactured product. For decking you can use Underlayment Exterior, A-C Exterior, or B-C Exterior, in descending order of quality. Indoor-outdoor carpeting, floor tile, or some other exterior-type wearing surface should always be used over the plywood.

Another type of plywood, High-Density Overlay (HDO) with nonslip face, needs no other wearing surface. HDO has a hard impregnated-fiber surface. Its color may fade somewhat in outdoor exposure, be warned. Medium-Density Overlay (MDO), is the grade to use if you want a smooth, painted surface.

APA grade-trademarked plywood—and this is the only kind you should buy—comes stamped with a group number indicating species. As with other decking lumber, Group 1 is the stiffest. Half-inch thick Group 1 plywood will span 16 inches with

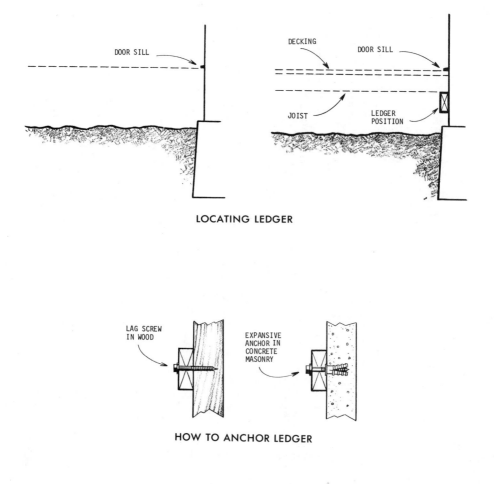

DOOR SILL

DECKING   DOOR SILL

JOIST   LEDGER POSITION

LOCATING LEDGER

LAG SCREW IN WOOD

EXPANSIVE ANCHOR IN CONCRETE MASONRY

HOW TO ANCHOR LEDGER

its face grain across the supports. You can get plywood designed to span 48 inches. It's 1⅛ inch thick and comes with tongue-and-groove edges for inter-panel support. The stuff is called 2-4-1 Exterior Underlayment.

STRUCTURE DESIGN. You need not be an engineer or an architect to design a deck. The pre-engineered tables presented here make it easy. Check your local building department to see whether these tables are acceptable. If not, ask them for ones that are.

The size of each structural member of a deck depends on what species of wood it is, its grade, and its spacing from other members, which determine how much of the floor load it must carry. It also depends on the concentration of floor load. A floor loading of 40 pounds per square foot (psf) for live load (people), plus another 10 psf for dead load (the weight of the structure), is widely accepted. The accompanying tables are based on these figures. In heavy snow-load areas, a much heavier design would be required on unroofed decks.

The usual deck construction features vertical posts holding up horizontal beams. Deck planks rest across the beams. Some systems use joists between deck and beams. Often they can be eliminated.

Start designing with the planks you plan to use. Look in the plank table. How far will they span? Because all lumber comes in two-foot multiples—8, 10, 12, 14, 16 feet—try to arrange your spans to use full planks without wasteful trimming. Ideally, planks can be continuous over two or more spans, not just one. This builds in added strength.

Suppose you're planking with Southern pine 2 × 4s. According to the plank table, they'll span 60 inches, or 5 feet, between beams. You can order them in 10-foot lengths and plan on using each length continuous over two spans.

Next, figure for the beams. Consult the beam table for the species of beam lumber and the beam spacing. In the example, beam spacing was 5 feet (60 inches). Suppose that you plan to use Douglas fir beams. From the small table, you find this wood is in Species Group 1. The beam-span table shows that four sizes from 4 × 8 to 3 × 12 beams will work at a 5-foot beam spacing, giving beam spans from 9 to 12 feet. Choose the beam span that best suits the size of your deck. Take it at right angles to the planking, of course, because that's the direction the beams must run. If the deck is to be 10 feet wide, you could most economically use 3 × 10 beams placed every five feet on centers. You could also use heavier designs, but that wastes lumber.

The last thing to figure is for supporting posts. Calculate the floor load area to be supported by each post. This is easy. Just multiply the beam spacing (5 feet in the example) by the post spacing. Placing one post at each end of the 10-foot deck beams gives a post spacing of 10 feet. No need for more posts than that. So, 5 feet times 10 feet gives a floor load area of 50 square feet. For Douglas fir posts, you'd look under 60 (the next higher column) in the post table and see that 4 × 4 posts will handle anything up to 12 feet high.

That's your deck design, then: planks, beams, posts. All structurally sound. In studying the three tables, you'll soon note that you have quite a bit of leeway to feed economy of materials into your design. If by spacing the beams a little closer together, you can take advantage of a whopping lumberyard sale on less-strong spruce planking, you stand to save. Like income tax, though, figure it both ways to be sure.

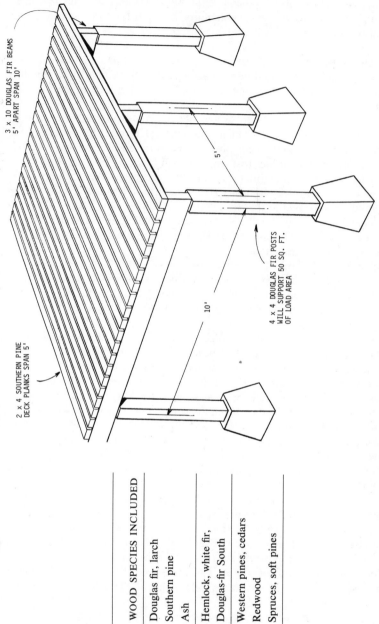

3 x 10 DOUGLAS FIR BEAMS
5' APART SPAN 10'

2 x 4 SOUTHERN PINE
DECK PLANKS SPAN 5'

5'

10'

4 x 4 DOUGLAS FIR POSTS
WILL SUPPORT 50 SQ. FT.
OF LOAD AREA

SPECIES GROUP	WOOD SPECIES INCLUDED
1	Douglas fir, larch Southern pine Ash
2	Hemlock, white fir, Douglas-fir South
3	Western pines, cedars Redwood Spruces, soft pines

PLANK SPANS

SPECIES GROUP	MAXIMUM SPAN						
	1 × 4	2 × 2	2 × 3	2 × 4	2 × 6	2 × 3 on edge	2 × 4 on edge
1	16"	60"	60"	60"	60"	90"	144"
2	14"	48"	48"	48"	48"	78"	120"
3	12"	42"	42"	42"	42"	66"	108"

(Construction grade or better)
From *Construction Guides for Exposed Wood Decks*, L. O. Anderson, T. B. Heebink, and A. E. Oviatt

BEAM SPANS

SPECIES GROUP	BEAM SIZE (in.)	BEAM SPACING (feet)								
		4	5	6	7	8	9	10	11	12
1	4 × 6	To 6' spans →	→	↑						
	3 × 8	To 8' spans →	→	→	→	↑				
	4 × 8	To 10' →	→	To 8' →	To 7' spans →	→	To 6' spans →	→	→	↑
	3 × 10	To 11' →	→	To 9' →	To 8' spans →	→	→	→	To 7' spans →	↑
	4 × 10	To 12' →	→	To 10' →	To 9' spans →	→	→	To 8' spans →	→	↑
	3 × 12		To 12' →	To 10' →	→	To 9' →	→	To 8' spans →		
	4 × 12			To 11' →	→	To 10' spans →	→	→	To 9' →	
	6 × 10				To 12' →	→	To 11' →	To 10' spans →	→	
	6 × 12						To 12' spans →	→		

(continued)

BEAM SPANS

SPECIES GROUP	BEAM SIZE (in.)	|← BEAM SPACING (feet) →|								
		4	5	6	7	8	9	10	11	12
2	4 × 6	To 6' spans →								
	3 × 8	To 7' spans →		To 6' spans →						
	4 × 8	To 9' →	To 8'	To 7' spans →		To 6' spans →				
	3 × 10	To 10' →	To 9'	To 8'	To 7' spans →	To 6' spans →				
	4 × 10	To 11' →	To 10'	To 9'	To 8' spans →	To 7' spans →	To 6' spans →			
	3 × 12	To 12' →		To 10'	To 9'	To 8' spans →	To 7' spans →	To 7' spans →		
	4 × 12		To 12' →	To 11'	To 10' spans →		To 9' spans →		To 8' spans →	To 6'
	6 × 10			To 12' →	To 11'	To 10' spans →	To 9' spans →	To 9' spans →		
	6 × 12			To 12' spans →				To 11' spans →		To 10'
3	4 × 6	To 6' spans →								
	3 × 8	To 7' spans →	To 6' spans →							
	4 × 8	To 8' →	To 7'	To 6' spans →						
	3 × 10	To 9' →	To 8'	To 7'	To 6' spans →					
	4 × 10	To 10' →	To 9'	To 8'	To 7' spans →	To 7' spans →				
	3 × 12	To 11' →	To 10'	To 9'	To 7' spans →	To 7' spans →	To 8' spans →			
	4 × 12	To 12' →	To 11'	To 10'	To 9' spans →		To 8' spans →	To 9' spans →	To 7' spans →	
	6 × 10					To 9' spans →		To 8' spans →	To 6' spans →	
	6 × 12			To 12' spans →	To 11' spans →			To 10' spans →	To 7' spans	To 8'

(No. 2 or Better; No. 2 medium grain Southern pine)

From *Construction Guides for Exposed Wood Decks,* L. O. Anderson, T. B. Heebink, and A. E. Oviatt

MINIMUM POST SIZES

SPECIES GROUP	POST SIZE (in.)	FLOOR LOAD AREA (sq. ft. on post)									
		36	48	60	72	84	96	108	120	132	144
1	4 × 4	To 12' heights →				To 10' heights →			To 8' heights →		
	4 × 6					To 12' heights →				To 10' →	
	6 × 6									To 12' →	
2	4 × 4	To 12' →		To 10' heights →			To 8' heights →				
	4 × 6			To 12' heights →			To 10' heights →				
	6 × 6						To 12' heights →				
3	4 × 4	To 12' →	To 10' →		To 8' heights →			To 6' heights →			
	4 × 6		To 12' →		To 10' heights →			To 8' heights →			
	6 × 6				To 12' heights →						

(Standard and Better grade for 4 × 4 posts; No. 1 and Better for larger sizes)

From *Construction Guides for Exposed Wood Decks,* L. O. Anderson, T. B. Heebink, and A. E. Oviatt.

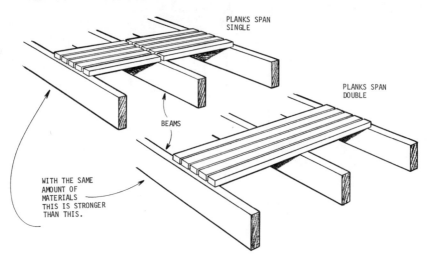

PLANKS SPAN
SINGLE

PLANKS SPAN
DOUBLE

BEAMS

WITH THE SAME
AMOUNT OF
MATERIALS
THIS IS STRONGER
THAN THIS.

DOUBLE PLANK SPAN IS STRONGER

Letting the beams or joists overhang their underpinnings is okay. The maximum is one-fourth the span. Decking can overhang slightly, too, but not more than a few inches.

FASTENERS. Joining one wood deck member to another calls for proper fasteners. Mostly, they will be nails, but also used are screws, Strapnails, framing anchors of various types, as well as bolts and lag screws. All fasteners used for deck construction should be of a nonrusting material—galvanized steel, usually—so they won't stain the decking members. If you prefer, screws may be used in place of nails for a tighter, but more costly, job.

A good nail rule is: long enough to penetrate the thicker backup member by twice the thickness of the thinner member, but never less than 1½ inch. For instance, you'd use 12-penny nails (3¼-inch long) to hold 2-inch deck planking to the beams. Nails should always be driven through the thinner member into the thicker one.

A good rule to screw length is: size the screw so that it will penetrate the receiving member at least the thickness of the thinner member, but never less than one inch. Use 3½-inch-long screws to hold down 2-inch deck planking, which is really 1½ inch thick.

Carriage bolts need washers only under their nuts. Machine bolts and lag screws need flat washers at head and nut ends to keep from crushing the wood. Lag screws should be installed with a washer. Always drill bolt holes the same diameter as the bolts. Drill pilot holes for screws and lag screws the size of the solid portion of the screw between threads.

BUILD A DECK. The actual construction of a wood deck starts with soil preparation. If the deck's on a slope, try to maintain the slope as nearly original as possible. Water should run off without erosion. If drain tiles are called for, install them in shallow ditches and lead the water off to a good dump spot or a dry well.

Control weed growth by applying commercial ground-poisoning weed killers. You can also do it with 4- or 6-mil polyethylene sheeting. Poke a few holes in the covering to let some water through and reduce runoff. Place the deck right over the sheeting.

Footings are usually 2-foot-square cast-concrete slabs placed 12 inches or more below the ground on good tight soil. They must also be below the frost line. Footings should be 4 inches thick. Make them of the same type of concrete mix as described for the concrete patio on page 78. Pressure-treated wood posts or poles may reach out of the ground from the footings. Instead of this, precast concrete piers may be placed on the footings to stick out of the ground at least six inches. Ordinary wood posts can rest on the piers with a square of asphalt shingle between as a moisture barrier.

Precast piers come in 8- and 12-inch sizes. The 8-inchers are fine for deck supports. Pier tops are made in several forms. Among them: wood-block-insert, dowel recess, and nailing strap. Posts can be nailed to the wood-block tops, doweled into the recessed tops or tied into the straps by nailing. Strap-type piers have the advantage of providing hold-down as well as support for the deck in a strong wind. Blocks and dowels are not desirable because they let water be in contact with the post bottom, a poor practice that encourages rot.

If the footings are shallow, the piers can simply be set on them in a position to receive the posts. Deep footings require coming up out of the ground with concrete in order to set untreated wood members. For this, a circular 8-inch hole with its bottom splayed out to about 2 feet square can be dug and filled to at least six inches (check code) above grade with concrete.

Posts are cut to length with all their tops level with each other to rest the beams on. A tube level is the best tool for establishing what's level from one end to the other of the deck area. A carpenter's level and long, straight board will work.

In placing beams on posts, the temptation is to toe-nail them by driving nails in at an angle through the beam into the post. This makes a weak connection that cannot resist twisting and wind liftoff. Instead, use 1 × 4 nailed-on wood cleats or steel tie-straps to connect posts and beams. Put one on each side held with four 8-penny no-rust nails in the end of each tie. You can also purchase preformed galvanized metal connectors for this purpose.

If the deck is more than 5 feet high, angle-braces made of 2 × 4s should be fastened to the posts to create a bridgework effect that keeps the deck from shaking laterally. If the deck is attached to the house, there is often no problem. But if it's free standing and its posts do not reach deep into the ground, you may notice some lateral shake. "W" braces made of lengths of 2 × 4 can be used if post spacing is eight feet or less; if longer, use 2 × 6 braces. Install the braces diagonally from the bottom of one post to the top of the next, then from the top of that post to the bottom of the next one and so on. Hold them with 3/8-inch lag screws or bolts and washers. Use one at each end of every brace. Make sure the brace ends are sawed off *vertically*—not horizontally. Horizontal end-grain surfaces collect moisture and encourage rotting. Where two "W" braces come together at posts, leave a slight space between them to allow air-drying after a rain.

DECKING. Lay out deck boards across the tops of the beams. When deck planking is laid flat, use two 12-penny no-rust nails—special deformed-shank nails—at each beam. When planking is laid on edge, use one 40-penny spike at each beam for 2 × 3s and one 5-inch-long wood screw at each beam for 2 × 4s. Pre-drill the planks to avoid splitting.

Space planks 1/8 to 1/4 inch apart to prevent binding during a rain. Also, allow a quarter-inch space between plank ends. Make end joints between planks over the center of a beam. On-edge planks used with 3-inch or narrower beams need to be fastened farther back from the end to prevent splitting. To do it, double up underneath,

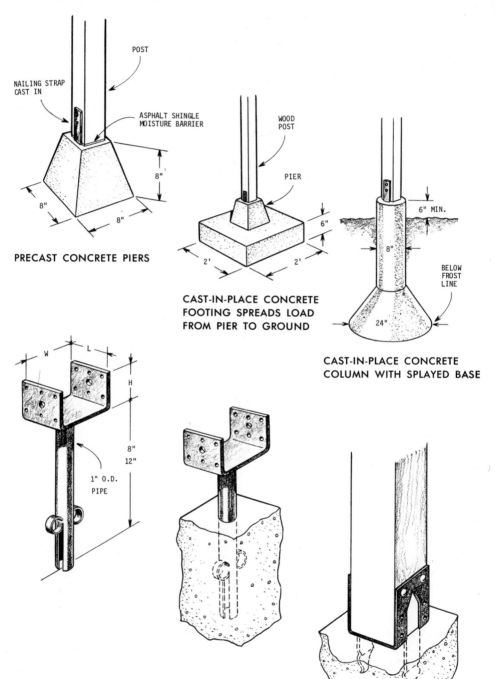

NAILING STRAP
CAST IN

POST

ASPHALT SHINGLE
MOISTURE BARRIER

8"

8"

8"

PRECAST CONCRETE PIERS

WOOD
POST

PIER

6"

2'   2'

**CAST-IN-PLACE CONCRETE
FOOTING SPREADS LOAD
FROM PIER TO GROUND**

6" MIN.

8"

BELOW
FROST
LINE

24"

**CAST-IN-PLACE CONCRETE
COLUMN WITH SPLAYED BASE**

W   L

H

8"
12"

1" O.D.
PIPE

SIMPSON POST BASES

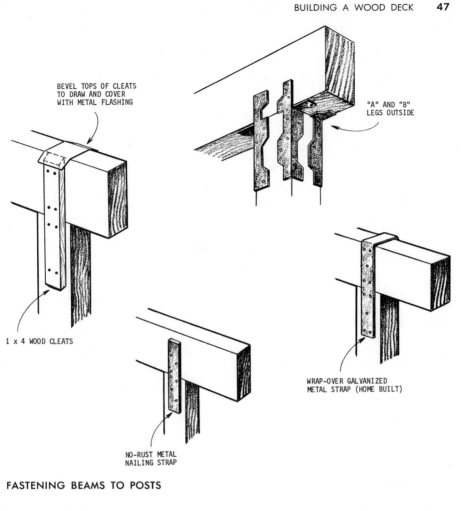

BEVEL TOPS OF CLEATS
TO DRAW AND COVER
WITH METAL FLASHING

"A" AND "B"
LEGS OUTSIDE

1 x 4 WOOD CLEATS

WRAP-OVER GALVANIZED
METAL STRAP (HOME BUILT)

NO-RUST METAL
NAILING STRAP

FASTENING BEAMS TO POSTS

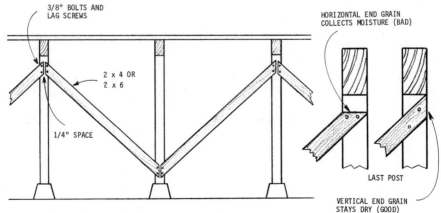

3/8" BOLTS AND
LAG SCREWS

HORIZONTAL END GRAIN
COLLECTS MOISTURE (BAD)

2 x 4 OR
2 x 6

1/4" SPACE

LAST POST

VERTICAL END GRAIN
STAYS DRY (GOOD)

"W" BRACING FOR LATERAL SUPPORT

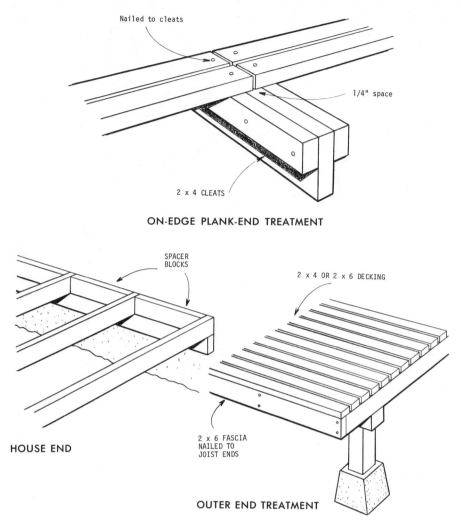

Nailed to cleats

1/4" space

2 x 4 CLEATS

ON-EDGE PLANK-END TREATMENT

SPACER
BLOCKS

2 x 4 OR 2 x 6 DECKING

HOUSE END

2 x 6 FASCIA
NAILED TO
JOIST ENDS

OUTER END TREATMENT

nailing 2-inch-thick wood cleats at each side of the beam top, providing a wide bear-ing area. Then fasten planks into the cleats, not into the beams (see the drawing).

On-edge planks with spans longer than 4 feet need spacer blocks nailed in the centers of the spans (see drawing). These give additional support from one plank to the next.

If any end joints tend to split when nailing, predrill slightly smaller than the nails.

If your combination of spans works out so that you have to cut planks in half or thirds to fit a span, you'll get the strongest deck by distributing the short, single-span planks alternately among all spans. Avoid putting the shorties all at one end of the deck. This end will be springier than the rest of the deck.

One more thing: place planks with their bark sides up. This way, when they're wet, they'll tend to curl downward and drain, not upward and collect water. The bark side is the convex side of the grain pattern as you view the board's end grain.

BUILDING A DECK

1. To build a deck, start at the ground. Dig holes below frost line and cast 2'-square concrete footings centered beneath each post. Then set precast concrete piers on top of the footings and backfill.

2. Cut the first post to proper level so that the finished deck will be the right elevation. Cut all other posts level with it. Place squares of shingling between each post and pier as moisture barriers.

3. The best piers come with steel straps cast into their tops so that the posts can be nailed. Nailing prevents later wind lift-off and keeps the posts from being loosened.

49

4. Set beams atop the posts. Distance between posts, beam dimensions, and type of lumber must agree with figures in charts on pages 39–43. Attach beams with cleats or straps, not by toenailing.

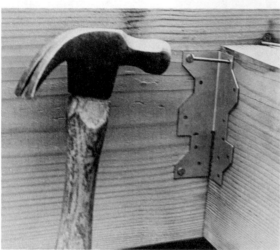

5. At the house end, beams may be hung from house framing with metal-framing anchors and nails. Most common type is this Simpson a34n anchor, which will support a floor's sheer load to some 310 pounds (140 kg) each.

6. When all the beams have been fastened in place, you can begin installing the planking. Space the planks with a nail between them to prevent contact when they swell.

7. At the edges, planks can extend beyond the last beam by several inches. To cut them off neatly, snap a chalk line from one end of the deck to the other so that no planks are missed.

8. Saw off the planks at the chalk line. The easiest way is with a power saw. Done by hand, it's a lot of work. If you're careful to split the line with the saw, you can get a perfect edge.

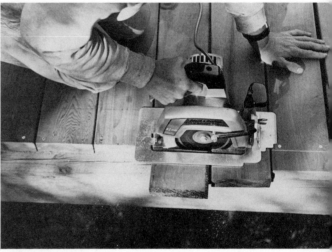

9. Posts for railings are held by drilling ⅜″ (9mm) holes through them and the deck supports, then fastening with ⅜″ (9mm) bolts. Clamp the posts in position and plumb them first. Notches shown for bottom railing are not recommended for wet climates.

51

10. Finished deck can be roofed over if desired by supporting the roof on posts at one end, on the house at the other. If deck height is more than 18 inches (0.5m), it should have a railing.

PRESERVATIVES. Unless you build your deck with rot-resistant wood, such as cypress, cedar, or redwood, steps should be taken to keep the deck parts from decaying. Some of these steps have already been described. More is needed, especially in wet climates. Dip all ends of boards into a pentachlorophenol water-repellent wood preservative before assembling the deck. Repeat the treatment subsequently each year, using the wood preservative on a brush. Flood it well into the wood. Better yet, you can dip whole boards before deck assembly. At least, flood preservative on them with a paintbrush.

Provide no-rust metal flashings to catch water wherever wood end grain is exposed horizontally, such as at deck posts. Or you can angle-cut the tops to slope them for better drainage.

Apply outdoor-type rubberized construction adhesive to the beam tops before planking. This comes in 11-fluid-ounce caulking cartridges for handy application as you go.

If the deck is more than about 18 inches above the ground, it should have a railing around it (check your code). However you build it, the supports must be strong enough to prevent a person from crashing through. A common spec is 20 pounds per linear foot of sidewise load. Some codes also require that the railing be designed so that a 9-inch-diameter ball (the size of a baby's head) cannot fit through at any point. Normal heights are up to about 42 inches above the deck.

In some railings, the deck-support posts are simply extended above the deck and horizontal members attached to them. These may also support bench-type seats. Railings should be able to support at least 20 pounds per linear foot. Railings using 2 × 4 top rails need posts spaced at 6-foot intervals or closer. Those with 2 × 6 top rails can take 8-foot spacing of posts.

Posts may also be bolted to beams. Make them of 2 × 6s for spacing of less than four feet; 2 × 8s or 4 × 4s for spacings to six feet. Fasten them with a pair of ⅜-inch bolts through both post and beam. Be sure to space the bolts as far apart as you can for leverage. Leave a ⅛- to ¼-inch space between floor boards and posts to allow the wood to dry.

Simple on-ground deck of spaced 2 × 4 planks set on nonrotting 2 × 4 runners below rests on a sand or pea-gravel sub-base. Squares left out can be used as planters, sandbox, etc.

Concrete piers, cast in place, can be used to support a wood deck. Dig below frost line, splay out the bottom with a shovel for a broad footing, then pour concrete into roofing-paper form tied with string.

Nail beams to drilled steel straps cast into the top of the columns. Folded roofing-paper pad protects wood spacer block from moisture damage. Spacer block was used to level beam with the tallest column.

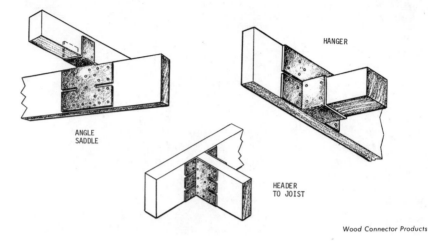

ANGLE
SADDLE

HANGER

HEADER
TO JOIST

Wood Connector Products

ONE FLAT PLATE CAN DO THESE JOBS

Serrated square-shanked nails give more holding power, reduce wood splitting. They resist the tendency to work loose and are great for deck-building.

A good way to treat planking is to dip it in a trough of penta preservative. Small can is used to flood preservative over the wood. Trough can be made from a length of rain gutter with two end caps sealed on.

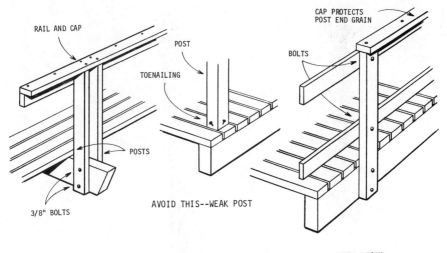

RAIL AND CAP

POST

TOENAILING

POSTS

3/8" BOLTS

AVOID THIS--WEAK POST

ACROSS BEAM ENDS

CAP PROTECTS
POST END GRAIN

BOLTS

WITH BEAMS

RAILING TREATMENTS

MORE NO-ROT MEASURES. Posts at beam ends may be doubled and bolted on each side of the beam, using long through-bolts.

- Don't simply nail post bottoms to the deck. It makes a weak railing and subjects the end grain to water and rot.
- Top rails should be designed to protect the end grain of the posts from rain water. The drawings show how, using a cap rail. Note how nailing into end grain is avoided, as it always should be.
- Don't let rails touch at their end joints, but keep them spaced for drying.
- Bottom rails are best mounted to posts without cutting into the posts as is often done. Bolt a cleat to the posts, then screw the rail onto it. Or use no-rust metal connectors or angle-irons to make the connection between posts and rails.
- Painting your new deck should be avoided. It's much better to treat it to a penetrating wood stain. These widely available finishes are *in* the wood, not on it, and won't crack, chip, or peel like paint. They far outlast paint, too. To renew them, sim-

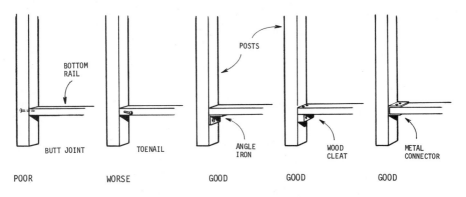

BOTTOM
RAIL

POSTS

BUTT JOINT

TOENAIL

ANGLE
IRON

WOOD
CLEAT

METAL
CONNECTOR

POOR   WORSE   GOOD   GOOD   GOOD

BOTTOM-RAIL FASTENINGS

Wire mesh, in 2-by-4-inch pattern, makes a good railing covering to keep small children from crawling through and falling. It's much easier than making numerous wood balusters.

Wood-baluster railing looks better than the mesh one. Wider posts are bolted onto beam, narrower in-between balusters are drilled and nailed. All tops are sloped to drain.

ply clean and recoat. You can get them in lightly pigmented (transparent) or heavily pigmented (opaque) forms. If you want the wood grain to show through, use transparent stain. If not, use opaque stain. Many reputable manufacturers produce both types in a wide variety of tones, light to dark. Check Olympic, Behr, Cabot, Sears, and Wards. Light, transparent stains are best for decks because traffic areas change less with wear. You can combine that with a matching color in opaque stain for the beams and posts in nontraffic areas.

• If you must paint, first coat everything with penta preservative. After it's dried thoroughly, follow with a coat of primer, then two coats of color. The planking, if painted, should receive a good porch and deck paint.

5 Building a Paver Patio

ONE OF THE EASIEST PATIOS to build is done with bricks, blocks, stones, or precast concrete tiles. This patio paving is easy because you can tackle a lot of work or a little, depending on how you feel and how much time you have. Also, you can do it either formally or informally. A formal job is complete with cast-in-place concrete base and rigid setting of paver units in mortar. An informal job goes with the mortarless method of setting, and loose joints. For specifics on how to build the concrete base, see the next chapter. Don't worry about finishing the concrete because the pavers — whatever type you use — will cover the underlying concrete.

To find out which pavers are available, visit local brickyards and concrete-products suppliers. Sometimes building-materials dealers handle bricks, plus precast concrete blocks and tiles. There you can look at everything in one place.

Pavers used in freeze-thaw climates must be able to take weathering. All concrete tiles and blocks can do it, and most stones can, but not all clay bricks will. Ask your dealer. In general, paving bricks can take weathering. Bricks intended for laying up into walls should be of the hard-burned, severe-weathering type for freezing-climate use as pavers. In mild climates any bricks may be used successfully on the ground.

One problem when using ordinary building bricks to make a mortarless patio is that the units aren't designed as pavers. They are not exactly half as wide as they are long. Thus they cannot be laid in mortarless basketweave and certain other patterns where widths are laid on lengths and must come out even. For a mortarless brick patio you'll either have to use paving bricks or lay building bricks in patterns that do not match two widths against one length. Running and stacked bonds work well with any bricks. So do diagonal-laid bond patterns. In any case, choose bricks without holes in them, or lay them on edge.

MORTARLESS PAVING. Whatever you do, design the width and length of your paver patio to come out even in the units you're going to use. You should thus settle on those before going ahead with anything else. If you use stone, no problem: Cut the stones to fit as you go.

Mortarless patios are much less work. Where traffic will be light and you don't want a formal appearance, use this method. To build the low-cost mortarless patio, start by outlining the area to be paved with 1 × 2 temporary stakes and stringlines. The exact method described is suggested by Brick and Tile Service of North Carolina.

First, dig out all grass and roots in the area, ending up with the bedding sloped away from the house to drain about ⅛ to ¼ inch per foot (10 to 20mm per m). Dig out to a depth of ½ to two inches (10mm to 50mm) deeper than the thickness of the bricks to be used. This allows for a smooth sand bedding to be added. The deeper the bedding, the better the drainage provided. In dry areas, choose the minimum; in wet areas go for the whole two inches.

A brick patio made by the easy mortarless method becomes an outdoor living room. Loose-laid brick makes a permanent, weatherproof surface. No bricklaying skills are required.

Brick Assn. of North Carolina.

No-mortar brick paving is set in a sand base with pavers set on edge or on end at the sides to keep bricks from spreading. Maintain this type of patio by removing loose-laid units.

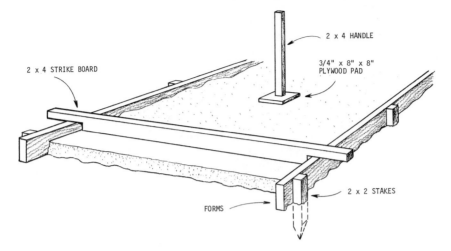

2 x 4 HANDLE

3/4" x 8" x 8"
PLYWOOD PAD

2 x 4 STRIKE BOARD

2 x 2 STAKES

FORMS

TAMPING AND LEVELING SAND BASE

Smooth the area and frame two adjacent patio edges either with leave-in redwood 2 × 4s and redwood stakes, or with rows of bricks set on edge. Place the bricks in ditches cut about two inches (50mm) deeper than the rest of the area. Align the edge bricks with your stringlines and tamp them in place with a hammer and block of wood.

When the two edges are finished as far as you're going with them, begin spreading sand over the ground deep enough so that when the pavers—bricks, blocks, tiles, stones—are laid flat in it, they will come up even with the brick edging. Smooth the sand with a straight board. Next, roll out a layer of 15-pound asphalt-saturated roofing paper over the sand bedding to discourage grass and weeds, and to help smooth out the sand. (This step is sometimes omitted and the pavers are set directly on the sand, but dollars are saved at the expense of more maintenance later.)

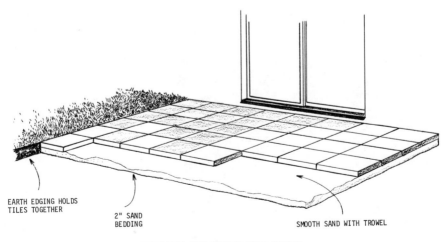

EARTH EDGING HOLDS
TILES TOGETHER

2" SAND
BEDDING

SMOOTH SAND WITH TROWEL

PRECAST CONCRETE TILE PATIO

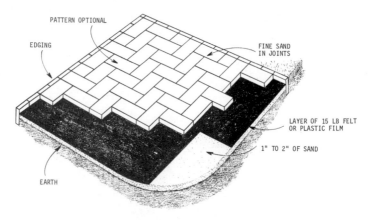

PATTERN OPTIONAL

EDGING

FINE SAND
IN JOINTS

LAYER OF 15 LB FELT
OR PLASTIC FILM

1" TO 2" OF SAND

EARTH

MORTARLESS BRICK PAVING

Loose-laid mortarless pavers give an informal appearance, especially when laid with color variations, as here. Concrete tiles are set in a basketweave pattern for a large patio.

Portland Cement Assn.

Flagstones are cut to fit by tapping a line across them with a mason's hammer. Using the chisel-printed end, keep tapping harder and harder until the stone breaks along the line. Stone makes the most elegant patio of all.

Beginning in one corner, lay pavers away from it according to your chosen pattern. For a running bond, start by laying a row of full units. Begin the second row with a half unit before laying whole units. Start the third row with a whole unit, the fourth with a half, and so on.

When you finish all the pavers for the whole length and width of your patio, complete laying brick edging for the other two sides of the patio. As before, these go about two inches deeper than the pavers. The purpose of the edging is to keep the pavers from spreading out. With the mortarless method, it is necessary. A redwood edging serves the same purpose.

If you like, you can sift dry sand into the tiny cracks between the pavers or leave them open. Should freezing weather heave up part of your patio, you can lift the too-high units out in the spring, scoop out some sand, and re-lay them to the original grade. A well-drained spot should be free of excessive frost-heaving.

The step-by-step photos show how a precast-concrete tile patio was built using the mortarless method. It uses an earth edging.

MORTAR METHOD. A mortar-set patio with concrete base is a permanent structure, good enough for an interior surface. It drains off the edges like a concrete patio and needs no maintenance. Any concrete patio can be made into a brick or stone patio using the mortar-set method.

To make a formal mortared-in patio is more work, of course. You must cast the concrete base and mortar the pavers as you lay them. Basically it's a concrete patio with a brick, block, stone, or tile finish.

Decide what elevation you want for the top of the patio. Subtract the thickness of your pavers, plus about half an inch for mortar, plus the three-inch (75mm) thickness of the concrete base. Then you can figure the depth to dig. In poorly drained soils, a gravel subbase may be needed (see the next chapter). Form for the concrete base and cast it the same as described in the next chapter. It should slope away from the house for good drainage.

If you want your pavers outlined by leave-in redwood forms, use forms high enough to reach up flush with the tops of the pavers. Otherwise, form the edges with ordinary 2 × 4s and remove them once the base has cured. Strike the concrete base off half an inch below the bottoms of the pavers. Contraction joints are needed in the base slab and up through the pavers, the same as for a concrete patio (see page 81). The amount of concrete required can be figured from the accompanying table.

MATERIALS NEEDED

AREA (l × w) (sq. ft.)	3" CONCRETE (cu. yd, including 10% waste)	BRICKS, BLOCKS						MORTAR MIX (60-lb. bags, including 10% waste)
		3¾" × 8"	Mortarless 4" × 8"	8" × 16"	3¾" × 8"	Mortared 4" × 8"	8" × 16"	
50	0.5	240	225	57	200	189	53	6
100	1.0	480	450	113	399	377	106	11
200	2.0	960	900	225	798	753	212	22
300	3.0	1440	1350	338	1196	1130	318	33
400	4.0	1920	1800	450	1595	1506	424	43
500	5.0	2400	2250	563	1993	1883	530	54

BUILD A PAVER PATIO

1. To set pavers over an old patio, you need not cast a concrete base. Instead, spread the base concrete as you lay each paver. Here a stiff sand-mix is shoveled down.

2. Set the pavers on the sand-mix concrete without dropping them into it. Pavers may be bricks, precast-concrete tiles like these, concrete blocks, or flagstones.

Cement and Concrete Assn. of England

3. Tap the tile down flush with the rest of the patio. The stringline along the patio edge permits laying it to the proper slope, even though the old patio was improperly graded.

4. The finished patio looks much improved over the old one. Varying the sizes of the units gives an ashlar appearance with no lengthy point lines to draw the eye.

Instead of finishing off the base concrete smoothly, roughen it with a broom and leave it. This provides a better bond for the subsequent mortar layer.

Laying of the pavers can start as soon as the base is finished, or it can wait a week or more. At any rate, don't walk on the base for several days—until it hardens sufficiently. If you don't set pavers immediately, cover the base with polyethylene sheeting to damp-cure for several days.

Mortar Mixing. The easiest way to get mortar for bedding of pavers is with ready-packaged mortar mix. You can buy it in 60-pound bags with all the ingredients but water. The bag tells you how much water to add and how to mix. Mix in a wheelbarrow or purchased mortar box, using enough water for a nice spreading consistency. Mortar quantities are shown in the table.

Use a bricklayer's trowel, one that's somewhat triangular and measures about 4½ inches (115mm) across at the heel of the blade and is about 10 inches (250mm) long, heel to toe. Spread mortar roughly half an inch deep so that when your pavers are set flat in it, they can be tapped down with the handle of the trowel to the desired level. Spread enough for several pavers in one corner and work away from there. As you lay each subsequent paver, butter its joining edges with mortar and shove it against the previously laid one. Tap it toward the other pavers until they are half an inch apart. Try to keep mortar off the exposed faces.

Keep going for an hour or so, then go back and tool the stiffening mortar joints between pavers. Use a bricklayer's jointing tool or a short length of ³/₄-inch (20mm) copper pipe to make a smoothly rounded concave joint between each paver. If you'd rather, you may simply slice off mortar above the pavers and leave flush joints.

Mortar that stiffens because of air-drying may be saved by adding water and remixing. This is called *retempering*. Mortar that is more than 2½ hours old has begun to set and should be discarded.

Bricks laid as pavers should be wetted, but left to surface-dry before laying. Precast concrete and stones should not be wetted before laying.

The day after you finish your formal patio, you can remove the mortar stains from the pavers with a mild acid wash. Add one part commercial strength muriatic acid to 10 parts water and brush the solution onto the patio. Wear rubber gloves, old clothes, and goggles to protect yourself from the acid. Scrub over any thickly mortar-coated areas with a brush to help remove the deposits. When the acid bubbling stops, hose off the spent acid, keeping it out of flowerbeds. Stone patios should be given a detergent scrubbing instead of an acid-wash to clean mortar from them; acids tends to stain the stones.

Don't walk on the patio for a week after the final mortaring, to give the joints time to harden fully. After that you can begin enjoying it.

CEMENT-TREATED SUBBASE. An easy half-way measure between the mortarless and mortar methods may be used instead. Instead of a plain sand bedding for the pavers, add one part portland cement to 10 parts clean sand and mix. Spread and level it. Lay your pavers on it without mortar. The cement-treated bedding will set up hard to provide excellent support.

A variation on this method is shown using ready-packaged sand-mix concrete (see the photos). It makes a subbase strong enough for use with mortared brick pavers. Soil-cement may also be used as a subbase. See the chapter covering it.

If spreading mortar on pavers doesn't appeal to you, it can be avoided on patios with cement-treated subbases this way:

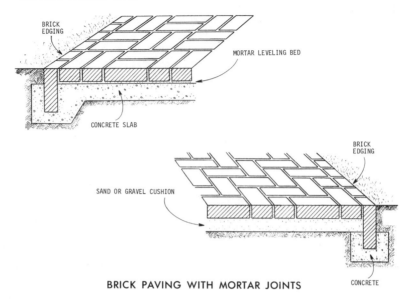

BRICK EDGING

MORTAR LEVELING BED

CONCRETE SLAB

BRICK EDGING

SAND OR GRAVEL CUSHION

CONCRETE

BRICK PAVING WITH MORTAR JOINTS

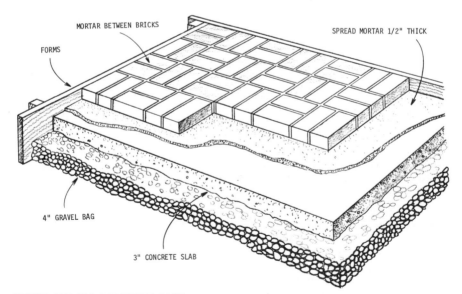

MORTAR BETWEEN BRICKS

SPREAD MORTAR 1/2" THICK

FORMS

4" GRAVEL BAG

3" CONCRETE SLAB

BRICKS SET ON CONCRETE BASE

Lay the pavers with ½-inch (12mm) joints around each. Then mix up a sand-cement filler, using one part portland cement to two parts clean, fine mortar sand. Mix and spread dry over the patio, sweeping it into all joints. Tamp it down tightly into each joint using the edge of a piece of ⅜-inch (9mm) plywood. Sweep around until all joints are full, then remove any excess. Finally spray the patio with a garden hose to dampen, but not soak, all the joints. The filler will soon set up hard, shrinking slightly below the tops of the pavers.

BRICK PATTERNS

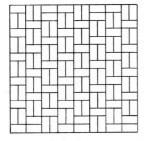

STAGGERED BASKET WEAVE

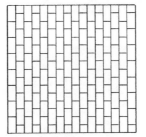

RUNNING BOND

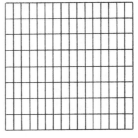

STACKED BOND

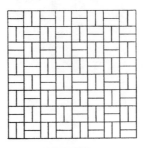

RUNNING BASKET WEAVE

BASKET WEAVE

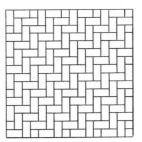

HERRING BONE

BUILD A BRICK PATIO

1. You can use many variations of the mortar and mortarless methods of paving. These step-by-step photos show how to make a brick patio with cement-treated subbase. First excavate and form the exposed edges.

2. Set edging bricks, buttering one end of each and laying it against the end of the last-placed brick. Each edge brick is set in a bed of mortar. Wood form aligns edges.

3. With the area outlined, pour in gravel-free Sakrete sand-mix (some manufacturers call it topping). One 60-pound bag will cover about 3 sq. ft. 2" deep. No water is used.

4. Make a leveler and smooth the subbase out one brick's thickness below the edge bricks. Moisture from the ground will soon soak into the sand-mix and harden it.

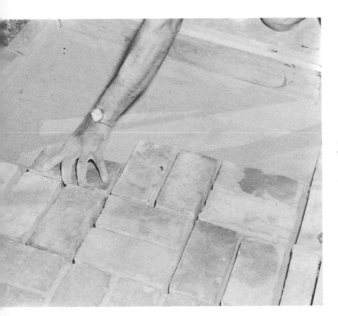

5. Set each brick firmly down on the subbase leaving ½″ (12mm) joints around it. Bricks should come even with the top of the edging.

6. Mix mortar using Sakrete mortar mix and water. Pack some mortar into every joint and smooth each off flush with the surface. Mortar should fill the joint completely.

7. When the mortar stiffens enough so that a water film does not come to the surface when you tool it, run every joint with a bricklayer's jointing tool. You can leave the joints flush if you wish.

8. The finished, cleaned surface looks formal as though it had a concrete base. This easy method is suitable for small or large paved surfaces.

6 | How To Make Attractive Concrete

MOST PATIOS ARE MADE OF CONCRETE. And most of these are smooth-troweled and natural gray in color. The only thing recommending this treatment is low cost. We recommend that you consider putting both color and texture into a do-it-yourself concrete patio. It will look better and stand apart from others.

You have your choice from among any of the concrete colors and stains: white, reds, pastels, browns, yellows, oranges, beiges, and even blue and green, though those colorings often cost lots more.

You also have your choice from among numerous textures. A steel trowel gives a slick texture. A magnesium float used as the final finish gives a grittier one, better than wet for its nonslip footing. A sponge-rubber float makes a still coarser finish. Exposed aggregate leaves attractive stones in view at the concrete's surface. These can be practically anything that you can get your hands on to either mix in or spread over the fresh slab before it sets.

Troweling rock salt into the surface before it hardens makes it pockmarked all over. Brooming it gives it lines of texture in the direction of the brooming. Spatter-dashing, then troweling lightly, gives a travertine marblelike texture.

Pattern-stamping can make your concrete look like brick, stone, or tile without the cost and work of laying these. Later, we'll tell how to produce each of these finishes so you can thus put the best face on your patio.

USING CONCRETE. You can tackle a patio-building project all at once or divide it up into sections and take on a section at a time. If you'll need less than about one cubic yard of concrete—the equivalent of a yard wide, a yard long, and a yard deep— you might mix it yourself with a rented concrete mixer. This requires that you know something about making good concrete.

First of all, assemble the materials: Type 1 or Type 2 portland cement, sand, and gravel or crushed stones. The cement is available from your building-materials dealer in 94-pound bags containing one cubic foot of cement each. (In Canada bags of cement weigh 80 pounds and hold about 7/8 cubic foot.) The cement acts as a glue to bind the sand and cement particles together. Do not make concrete with "plastic cement" or "masonry cement." These are unsuitable.

Sand for concrete should be clean and free of silt. Specify that you want "concrete sand." This contains various particle sizes from dust all the way up to about 1/4-inch (6mm) chunks.

The stones should contain variable-sized particles, too, from 1/4 inch (6mm) up to a maximum size of 1 inch (25mm) for most patios. They, too, should be clean. They should also be sound so they won't break up when exposed to freezing and thawing. When you buy them, specify that they're for concrete-making.

Concrete patios can be much more than the plain gray ones you see so often. The extra effort to make exposed aggregate and other interesting textures is mostly in their planning.

Proportion your materials using either "Mix A" or stronger "Mix B" as shown in the table of mixes. Which you should use depends on patio thickness. Use Mix A for 3-inch (75mm) and thicker projects. Use Mix B for thin-section ones.

Concrete is mixed one batch at a time in the mixer. Use the proportions in the table on page 91.

While you may proportion materials by counting out shovels of it, a better way is to measure out pails the first time, counting the total number of shovels of each material it takes to fill the pail. Then follow those proportions in subsequent shovel-batching.

Use this method of batching the mixer: Put in about half the water, then half the stones. Add all the sand, then all the cement, and put in the rest of the stones. Finally, add the rest of the water.

Don't overload the mixer drum. A full load is about 60 percent of its rated volume. The mix should be uniform in color and should plop neatly from the mixer blades without being soupy. Watch how you peer into the rotating drum, though, or you might get a painful eyeful.

Your concrete mix should contain as little water as possible yet be what's called *workable*. If it's too stiff to work well, you can add more water and mix again. If it's too soupy, you'll have to add more cement, sand, and stones in correct proportions and remix to dry it up. Soupy concrete is weak and cannot make a satisfactory job. The amount of moisture carried by the sand makes a difference, so make the hand-squeeze sand test shown in the photos.

Rented concrete mixer towed home behind your car lets you mix concrete up to about one cubic yard a day per person.

Once you get the correct proportion of water, stick with it all the way through the project, so long as the sand's moisture content stays the same and the concrete remains workable without being runny. Dump the concrete into a rubber-tired contractor's wheelbarrow and haul it to the patio site for use.

After the last batch has been dumped, clean everything, including the mixer. Use water and a wire brush, if necessary, to get all the hardening mix off. Shovel a pail of gravel into the rotating drum and add some water to clean it.

Have your concrete mixer and piles of materials arranged to keep waste motions to a minimum. For safety, don't put anything into the turning drum except the concrete ingredients. Keep your hands and shovels out.

MIX YOUR OWN CONCRETE

1. Make this test to see whether the sand you will use is clean enough for making concrete. Fill a jar half full of sand, fill with water and shake. Let it settle overnight, then measure the thickness of the top silt layer. If it's less than ⅛" (3mm), the sand is okay to use.

2. Sand's moisture content varies. Squeeze-test yours so you'll know how much water to use in your mix. Dry sand (left) holds no surface moisture. After squeezing, it comes apart in your hand. Average damp sand (center) stays in a tight wad after squeezing. It adds a little water to the mix. Wet sand (right) leaves your palm wet after squeezing. When using it, the mix water should be reduced a quart or two per batch.

3. The amount of water in the mix determines how easily it will work and how strong it will be. These are opposites, making the amount of mix water a compromise. The mix at the left is too wet and runny. The one at the center is just right. At the right, the mix is too stiff to work easily. It needs more water.

4. While the table on page 91 gives good starting proportions for sand and stones, the exact ones you use will depend on the materials you have. Adjust your mix according to these photos. Left is too sandy. Its stones don't show. Add more stones. Center is correct combination of sand, stones. Right is too stony. There's not enough sand to fill in between the stones. Add some sand.

5. Batch your water into the mixer carefully in cans. This 5-gallon can is fine for the job. Use a separate pail for the dry ingredients.

Ready-Packaged Mix. You have another option of mixing concrete for a patio project — use sacked concrete. The sacks are sold by building-materials dealers. They contain correctly proportioned cement, sand, and stones. All you do is add the amount of water called for on the bag and mix. The concrete produced is often stronger than you could make by buying and proportioning the ingredients yourself. You should stick to nationally known brands, such as Sakrete, or buy local brands known to make good concrete.

Ready-packaged mixes are best for small projects of less than a cubic yard. For large projects they are costlier than buying separate materials and combining them yourself. Be sure that you get gravel mix, sometimes called *concrete mix*. Sand mix, also called *topping*, contains no stones and is thus not a very efficient material.

Sacked-concrete mixes come in 30-, 45-, 60-, or 90-pound bags ready to use. A 90-pound bag makes about ²/₃ cubic foot of concrete, 40 bags make a cubic yard.

There is no air-entraining agent in ready-packaged mixes, so avoid using them in freezing climates. Same with concrete that you proportion and mix yourself.

Whenever you use concrete, plan on having some 10 percent extra to allow for miscalculations and waste. It's better to have a little extra than to run short and end up with a low spot in your patio that collects water during every rain. The table on estimating volume allows for this.

Ready-Mix. If you'll be needing more than a few cubic yards of concrete at one time, it pays to use ready-mixed concrete. All you need do is call up your ready-mix producer and tell him how much you want. He delivers it to you in a large truck-mixer.

You should also specify:

- When you need it;
- Maximum-size aggregate (1-inch) (25 mm);
- That it contain at least six bags of cement per cubic yard (8 bags per cubic meter) (m³);
- That it contain no more than six gallons (23 l) of water per bag of cement.

These figures are important. Your ready-mix dealer understands what they mean in terms of quality.

If you live in a freezing climate, you should also state that you want your ready-mix to be air-entrained. This means that an air-entraining agent is added to it before mixing. The agent traps billions of microscopic air bubbles in the mix. In the hardened concrete, these act as safety valves for pressures from freezing, expanding water inside the patio slab. They keep the slab from scaling off in pieces at the surface. The correct amount of air-entrainment is five to seven percent.

One more thing to tell your ready-mix man: Say that you want the concrete to arrive with a *slump* of about 4 inches (100mm). Slump is the professional's measure of the workability of concrete. Too much slump indicates weak, soupy concrete. Too little slump means that it will be hard to put in place and finish.

While you have no means of checking percentage of air-entrainment or slump on the job, at least you'll have asked for the right amounts of each.

When the truck-mixer arrives on the job, you should be ready with tools, wheelbarrow, wood-plank ramps, and helpers. Have at least two helpers for three cubic yards of mix. If the mix must be wheelbarrowed to the patio site, have two more helpers to do that.

Avoid placing concrete on a hot day when the sun will be shining on it. It sets up so fast under those conditions that you'll need double the number of helpers to keep up with it. Either start at dawn or wait until afternoon when the sun has passed. Likewise, don't place concrete on a day when the temperature is below 55° Concrete sets too slowly then, and you'd be up all night waiting to finish it.

Plan the route the ready-mix truck will use to reach your patio site. Avoid soft ground, sewer or septic piping, fragile sidewalk paving, and such. Where these obstacles cannot be avoided, lay down planks to prevent the truck from damaging them.

Organize the job to dump the whole truckload as quickly as possible. You have about three to five minutes of free unloading time per cubic yard. That's only 25 minutes or so for a 6-cubic-yard load. If you run over that time, you begin paying extra by the hour.

If for some reason, you cannot be ready on the day and time you say, be sure to call the ready-mix man and let him know in advance. Likewise, he should call you if he cannot make it as agreed.

If the ready-mixed concrete comes out of the mixer too stiff, you can have the driver add water and remix. Add no more than one gallon of water per cubic yard at a time (51 per m³). Have him mix for two minutes at full mixing speed, then test again. Remember that every gallon of water you add per cubic yard weakens the mix about 5 percent and increases the likelihood of cracking and scaling. Just don't be afraid to do it if the mix proves unworkable.

Ready-Mix Other Ways. Since a 3-cubic-yard project is the least practical for a ready-mix truck, other methods of getting concrete to your patio are worth considering. These let you handle a project in smaller steps, if you want. One is trailered ready-mix. A good many ready-mix dealers, as well as some building-materials dealers, offer small concrete mixers. These are self-dumping, yet they can be towed behind your car. At the rental plant, the correctly proportioned mix is fed into them — up to one cubic yard in one batch. It mixes as you drive home. You back up to the patio, dump, and return for another load. A haul-it-yourself job needs only two people — one to drive and one to place and finish. The cost is a little more than for ready-mix. The relatively light trailer won't harm your yard the way a large truck would. And it's convenient. But be sure to clean the mixer carefully after use to avoid a $10-plus cleaning charge.

Some trailers are merely dumping-type hoppers that do not mix as you go. Don't use them because as you bump along, the stones tend to settle out of the mix, weakening it unnecessarily.

Pumped Concrete. The very best way to use concrete at home is to hire a concrete-pumping contractor to be on the job when the ready-mix truck arrives. As the ready-mix truck dumps its load into the pump's hopper, the pump forces it through a 2-inch hose. Concrete comes from the end of the hose like toothpaste from a tube. You hold the hose and control exactly where and how much concrete is dumped. A switch lets you stop the flow.

No matter how hard your patio is to reach, the hose can get there, even through a window if necessary. It can go as far as 500 feet (150m) from the pump location and up or down 100 feet (30m) or more.

Nothing could be easier! You can pump-place enough concrete for a large patio in half an hour or less. No waiting time is incurred and you can get along with just one helper. The only drawback is the cost of pumping, which is still reasonable. Most pumping contractors charge a $40 to $60 minimum for the small 2-inch (50mm) pump. This includes pumping the first seven cubic yards. After that, the usual pumping charge is about $4 to $6 per additional yard.

The pump handles a stone size of up to ³/₈ inch (9mm). When you order a mix to be pumped, be sure to tell your ready-mix dealer that you want *grout and pump mix.*

This contains no stones larger than 3/8 inch. Slump can be as normally specified. The pump can handle any slump that you can.

To find a concrete-pumping contractor, look in the Yellow Pages under "Concrete Pumping Services." Be sure the man you hire has a 2-inch pump. Some have only larger pumps that cannot efficiently handle jobs less than some 50 cubic yards. The man you want uses a small machine.

PATIO DESIGN. Plastic concrete will form itself to whatever shape you build. Hardened, it retains that shape after the forms are removed. A concrete patio must be designed to withstand foot traffic, plus take exposure to the weather. It must also stand up under any ground movement caused by freezing and thawing.

Most concrete patios are built a nominal four inches thick because they're formed with 2 × 4 boards placed on edge. The exact thickness if 3½ inches (90mm), unless the subbase is dug out below the bottoms of the forms. No need for that, just so long as the full 3½-inch depth is provided all over. A patio needs control joints spaced no more than 10 feet (3m) apart. If they're spaced farther, in-between cracks will develop. It also needs what are called *isolation* joints placed at every adjoining wall and slab.

Control joints may either be cut into the fresh concrete during finishing, or created by leave-in, no-rot wooden form boards. Isolation joints may be made with leave-in form boards or with 3/8-inch-thick (9mm) impregnated-fiber joint material placed between the patio slab and the existing walls and slabs before casting the new concrete.

If you are careful about quality, you can make a patio thinner than a nominal 4 inches. I have gone as thin as 1½ inches (40mm) with success, and in a freezing climate, too. To get away with it, you'll have to section the patio up into much smaller pieces with control joints or the thin slabs will crack. Considerable concrete is saved over building at a 4-inch thickness, so you may find the extra jointing worth the saving. If so, try these maximum control joint spacings:

Thickness	Jointing
1½ inch	2 feet
(40mm)	(0.6m)
2 inch	3 feet
(50mm)	(1.0m)
3 inch	5 feet
(75mm)	(1.5m)

Remember, those are exact thickness, not nominal ones. Control joints may be tooled in or formed in. Control-joint minimum depth is always one-fourth the slab thickness, ½ inch on a 2-inch-thick slab (12mm on a 50mm slab).

Lots of codes call for using steel mesh in the center of a concrete-patio slab, to strengthen it and to prevent cracking. Forget the mesh unless you're required to use it. Only quality concrete and proper control jointing will prevent cracking. The mesh will merely hold together whatever cracks develop. It's money and steel wasted.

GRAVEL SUBBASE? Many codes call for the use of a 4-inch (100mm) layer of gravel beneath the patio to prevent frost-heave. In truth, the gravel is needed only in poorly drained soils, where water might collect underneath the slab to freeze and crack it. If you have such a soil, use the gravel subbase. The gravel layer must be drained either by sloping it away from the house or installing drainage tiles beneath it. If your soil doesn't turn to mud each year, you can lay the patio right on the ground.

1. When building a concrete patio, begin by forming it. First dig out the topsoil down to a good subgrade that slopes slightly away from the house for drainage.

FORMING A CONCRETE PATIO

2. Lay out the 2 × 4 side forms for your patio to a stringline sloped away from the house ¼″ per foot (20mm per m). Nail them to 2 × 2 wood stakes driven into the ground.

3. Form stakes can be braced by driving other stakes at an angle to rest against their tops. A nail will help hold. For easy release, coat the forms with engine drain oil.

Forms for your patio can be 2 × 4s well-staked into the ground with 1 × 4 or 2 × 2 wood stakes. Place stakes a maximum of four feet apart and nail the forms to them. Curved forms can be made from 1 × 4 stock; if necessary, you can drop to as thin as 1/4 × 4 hardboard or plywood for even sharper curves. Place form stakes inside and outside curved sections to hold them smoothly bent. As you place concrete, the inside stakes can be pulled out.

Use 1 × 4 stakes at laps in the form boards to hold them in alignment. Forms should be set to slope the patio away from the house 1/4 inch per foot (20mm per m). Smooth the subgrade to the right slab thickness and you're ready for the concrete.

FORMING CURVES

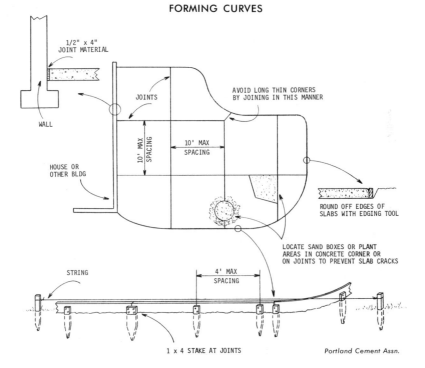

1/2" x 4" JOINT MATERIAL

WALL

JOINTS

HOUSE OR OTHER BLDG

10' MAX SPACING

10' MAX SPACING

AVOID LONG THIN CORNERS BY JOINING IN THIS MANNER

ROUND OFF EDGES OF SLABS WITH EDGING TOOL

LOCATE SAND BOXES OR PLANT AREAS IN CONCRETE CORNER OR ON JOINTS TO PREVENT SLAB CRACKS

STRING

4' MAX SPACING

1 x 4 STAKE AT JOINTS

Portland Cement Assn.

Cement and Concrete Assn. of England

4. Saw kerfs made in the 2 × 4 form boards at 2" intervals let them be bent smoothly around curves. While this shows the treatment for a sidewalk, a curved-edge patio is handled the same way. See next page for ways to form curves.

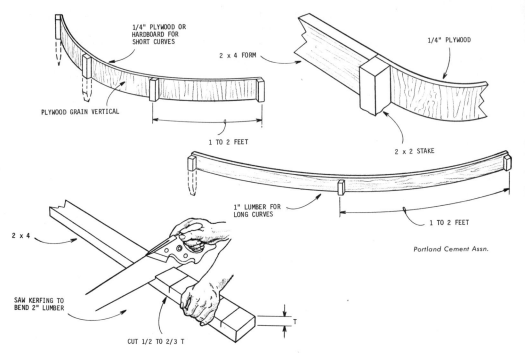

1/4" PLYWOOD OR HARDBOARD FOR SHORT CURVES

2 x 4 FORM

1/4" PLYWOOD

PLYWOOD GRAIN VERTICAL

1 TO 2 FEET

2 x 2 STAKE

1" LUMBER FOR LONG CURVES

1 TO 2 FEET

2 x 4

Portland Cement Assn.

SAW KERFING TO BEND 2" LUMBER

CUT 1/2 TO 2/3 T

T

ESTIMATING HOW MUCH. Figuring the quantities of materials you'll need to pave a patio is easy using the two tables on page 91. They'll work whether you use English or metric measure. Triangular areas are calculated as though they were squares, then the area is divided by two. Circular areas are figured at 3.14 times the circle's radius squared. For example, the area of an 18-foot-diameter circle is $3.14 \times 9 \times 9 = 254$ sq. ft. (the radius being 9 feet, half the diameter).

To figure free-form areas, draw them out to scale on square paper and count the number of squares. If each square represents one square foot, you have the area directly by counting.

Once you have the square-foot or square-meter area, look in the Estimating Volume Table under "cubic yards needed" or "cubic meters needed." Find the area figures that add up to your patio's total area and go down those columns until you come to the volume opposite the patio's design thickness. (Both inches and their approximate millimeter equivalents are shown.) The table gives the cubic yards and cubic meters required. Add to find your total requirement.

For example, suppose you're building a patio that's two inches thick and measures 11 feet by 50 feet. The total area is thus 550 square feet. Look in the table on the nonmetric (left) side under "cubic yards." The table shows that a 500-square-foot patio two inches thick needs $3\frac{1}{2}$ cubic yards of concrete, and a 50-square-foot one two inches thick needs $\frac{1}{3}$ yard. Adding these up gives a total of a little less than four cubic yards. Better order four cubic yards. It works the same way on the metric (right) side of the table.

Now that you know how much concrete you'll need, consult the other table, Estimating Materials. Both metric and nonmetric systems are shown. (If you're planning to use ready-mix, you can skip this table. Just ask for the amount of ready-mix that you need.) Decide whether to use Mix A or Mix B.

Suppose it's Mix A. Then, according to the table, for each cubic yard of Mix A, you'll need 21 cubic feet of stones, 15½ cubic feet of damp sand, and 6¼ bags of portland cement.

For your 4-cubic-yard patio you'd then need a total of 84 cubic feet of stones, 62 cubic feet of sand, and 25 bags of cement. Buy that much, proportion correctly, and you should come out about even on materials.

Sand and stones are normally sold either by the cubic yard or by the ton. To find cubic yards, simply divide cubic feet by 27. To find tons, figure up the weights, not the volumes of sand and stones, and divide each by 2000, which is the number of pounds per ton.

POURING. Meanwhile, back at the patio, you're ready to pour. Sprinkle the ground to keep mix water from migrating into the ground. Place concrete full depth against the forms. Spade along the sides to help settle it. Strike it off with a long, straight 2 × 4. Start at one end and seesaw the 2 × 4 along, moving it slightly toward the other end with each stroke. Fill in low spots with more concrete and go back over them. Leave a roll of concrete in front of the strikeoff. When you finish, go back over the slab a second time with the strikeoff to smooth the surface further.

As soon as you finish that, float the entire surface with a darby or bull float to remove major irregularities. Once is enough. Don't overwork the concrete. A slight amount of cement paste should work up to the surface, but not a lot. Remove and discard any stones that get in the way of finishing.

The next step is edging and jointing. Run an edger all around the slab. Form control joints throughout the slab as needed by running the tool against a flat 1 × 4 or 1 × 6 board laid flat on the slab. This gets them straight and neat.

FLOATING AND FINISHING. The timing of the next floating depends on whether you used air-entrained or plain concrete. With air-entrained concrete, water does not bleed to the surface and you can float it right away. With plain concrete, wait until the surface water has disappeared. If it lingers, help get rid of it by dragging a garden hose across the surface and off one edge.

Get out onto the slab on a pair of knee boards (see drawing) and work a wood hand float over the soft surface in wide, sweeping areas. Plan your moves to float over impressions left by the knee boards as you go. Run the edges and joints again while you're there. Wait until the water sheen leaves the slab before you do the final finishing. If it's by steel trowel, work the trowel in sweeping, overlapping arcs just as for floating.

For a roughened texture without float marks, drag a broom over the surface. A coarser texture is made by immediately using a stiff broom. A finer texture is made with a fine brush, later. Test to see what effect you want.

Finishing with a magnesium float makes an excellent patio surface. Start as soon as the water sheen leaves.

To use a sponge-rubber float, follow right after wood-floating, or else wait a while to create a smoother finish. Work the float in circles or arcs to make the texture you want.

All concrete should be cured to let it develop its full strength. Cure for four days in warm weather and for seven days or more in cool weather. You can do it by shoveling wet sand onto the surface, by flooding it continuously with a soaker hose or sprinkler, or by covering with a polyethylene plastic sheet. There are spray-curing compounds on the market. If your dealer has one, apply it as directed.

1. Dump concrete between the forms and strike it off with a long 2 × 4 straightedge. If you want a strong slab, work with it stiff like this, not soupy.

PLACING THE CONCRETE

2. Right after strikeoff, either bull-float or darby the surface all over to smooth the strikeoff marks. A long-handled bull float (shown here) lets you reach to all the parts of a large patio without your getting onto the soft surface.

3. Get on the surface with knee-boards and float it. Follow wood-floating with the first steel-troweling if a smooth finish is wanted. Work backwards to cover your knee-board impressions.

4. Edging and jointing of the patio should be done along with the first floating. Edging puts smoothly rounded corners all around. Cut control joints to regulate random cracking.

GETTING FANCY. Highly recommended for patios are the special effects that put the best face on your outdoor living. None require as much skill as steel-troweling to produce professional results.

Color — This may be put into or onto concrete by mixing in, dusting on, or staining. Mixing in is usually done in two courses to save money, though the one-course method won't prove costly if the color is dark gray or black. In this case, a concrete-coloring pigment is simply added to the concrete in the mixer. The resulting slab will be colored all the way through.

For the two-course coloring method, a plain base slab is cast and struck off about ⅝ inch (16mm) below the tops of the forms. Scratch that to provide "tooth" for the next course. The second course is mixed with portland cement, coloring pigment, and sand. No stones. It may be placed immediately, or after the base course has hardened. A bonding agent should then be brushed onto the base course before placing the colored topping. Bonding agents are widely sold for that purpose. A soupy mixture of portland cement and water may also be used as a bonding agent. Apply it with a brush to the dampened base slab.

Strike off and finish the topping course as for any concrete. Control joints must be continuous through both topping and base slabs. Leave-in wood forms do it easiest. Curing should not be with plastic sheeting because it causes spottiness in colored concrete.

To get pure colors, make the topping with white portland cement (it costs about double what regular cement does). Plain cement makes dirty colors. Don't make a sun-drenched patio very light-colored, though: You won't be able to stand it during the day.

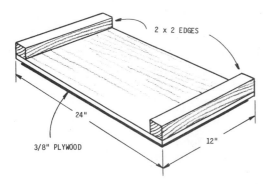

2 x 2 EDGES

KNEE-BOARD

24"

3/8" PLYWOOD

12"

1. Step by step, here's how to make a patio that shows its best face to the world. Start by grading out the area. A rented tractor saves lots of back-breaking work.

2. Do your finish-grading with the back of a rake or a straightedge nailed to a handle. Slope properly for good drainage. In poorly drained soils and freezing climates, a 4" gravel subbase should be used.

LAYING AN EXPOSED-AGGREGATE PATIO

3. Compact the surface hard with a hand tamper. This homebuilt one is made of a 2 × 6 nailed to a 2 × 2 wood handle. Dampen the subgrade to help in getting a solid base for your patio.

4. A money-saving 1½"-thick thin-section patio is made by assembling a ladder-like framework of leave-in 1 × 2 nonrotting form boards. Staggering the 2' squares lets short dividers be end-nailed. Secure with stakes.

5. Place concrete in the forms. Since this patio was not easily accessible to the ready-mix truck, a concrete-pumping service was used. Concrete flows from the end of the 2" hose like toothpaste from a tube.

6. Out in front of the house, the ready-mix truck dumps directly into the hopper of the portable concrete pump. Hose was snaked through the garage for access to the back-yard patio.

7. Nearing the end of the pour, the owner gets ready to press the remote "stop" button to cut the flow of concrete through the hose. Mix need not be this sloppy. Less water would have made a stronger job.

8. Whether you're pumping or placing concrete by hand, start against the form and work away from it to compact fresh concrete against what's already there. Special grout and pump mix contains no stones larger than ⅜" so it will pass through the pump.

9. Concrete-pumping contractor cleans up his equipment by running a garden hose onto the hopper and pumping a wet sponge through the hose. About two bushels of unusable mix comes out of the end.

10. Meanwhile, the patio owner gets busy striking off and finishing his project. A short strikeoff board was notched at the ends to leave each square ⅝" lower than the tops of the forms. This made room for an ag topping.

11. Scratching up the top of each base slab provides lots of "tooth" for the special topping layer placed later. A piece of folded-up chicken wire does the job quickly.

12. Before placing the colored exposed-ag topping course, the surface of the base course should get an application of bonding agent, here Weld-Crete, by Larsen Products, Rockville, Md. 20852. Topping may then be placed right away or much later.

13. Coloring pigment in handy premeasured 1-lb. bags is dumped into the mixer drum during batching of portland cement, attractive stones, and water. No sand was used in this topping mix.

14. Homeowner Chuck Kearns dumps a barrow load of colored topping containing pea gravel onto the bonding-agent-treated base course. Because the topping layer is only ⅝″ thick, a little topping mix goes a long way.

15. A short strikeoff board quickly levels the topping with the form tops. Light-gold-colored squares throughout the patio's center accent the dark brown ones around the edge. The same stones were used in both colors.

16. After strikeoff, only a light smoothing with a half-size mason's trowel was needed. Then the surface was left to begin setting up enough for aggregate exposure. This took about 1½ hours.

17. When the surrounding topping had set up enough to brush and water-flush without dislodging many stones, the garden hose and broom were put to work. Care was taken not to expose more than top third of stones.

18. After each mixing-pouring session, an immediate and thorough clean-up of all tools and equipment is necessary. Otherwise, hardening concrete clings to them and must be chipped off later.

Make up small test samples to determine the right proportion of coloring pigment. In general, fully saturated colors require 7-percent concrete-coloring pigment mixed in with the cement. Light tints take about 1½-percent coloring pigment. Never use more than 10-percent pigment: It weakens the mix too much. Use only pigments intended for use with concrete and mortar. Paint pigments will not work.

Dust-on coloring saves money because the color goes only into the top quarter inch or so. Buy a ready-mixed dust-on coloring compound or make your own, using two parts white portland cement, one part concrete-coloring pigment, and two parts fine mortar sand. Mix, dry, and shake it onto the surface just before wood-floating. Float it in; apply again in a second coat, and float again, then finish as usual. You'll need half a pound of dust-on mix per square foot of patio (8kg per m²).

Staining of concrete is done after the slab is at least six months old, better yet, a year. Use one of the commercially prepared inorganic stains (Kemiko is the largest-selling brand, made by Kemiko, Inc., 918 North Western Ave., Los Angeles, Calif. 90029.) You'll need a gallon for each 200 sq. ft. for two coats. You can also use oil-base stains designed for concrete. The most lasting job is done with the inorganic stain, though, because it actually changes the chemical composition of the surface concrete. Colored waxes help to prolong and smooth out the coloring effect. One gallon covers 600 to 900 sq. ft. One coat is enough. Kemiko, Inc. makes them, also.

Oil-base stains need frequent recoating. Alkali-resisting stains must be used. Ordinary wood stains have trouble with concrete.

Exposed aggregate. You will like exposed-ag. Select the stones to be exposed for their appearance as well as for their ability to stand exposure to the weather. If they are large (more than an inch) or expensive, use the spreading method; if they're small and cheap, use the mix-in method.

For the spreading method, make your concrete as usual, strike if off, darby, and wood-float it. If you want the mortar between the exposed stones to be colored, make the exposed-ag with colored concrete. Either the one- or two-course methods may be used. Before the concrete sets and as soon as it will support the pretty stones, sprinkle them by hand or shovel over the surface. Float in with a wood float, or tamp them in with the edge of a straight 2 × 4 only until they're flush with the mortar surface. Wait perhaps an hour for the surrounding concrete to begin setting. Then brush and water-flush some surface mortar away to expose the top third of the stones. If many exposed-ag stones are loosened during the brush/flush process, wait longer before finishing it. If adequate exposure is difficult, use a wire brush and hurry along —it's getting ahead of you.

The mix-in method of making exposed-ag concrete is usually done in two courses, the same as when making that kind of colored concrete. Mix the pretty stones right into the topping. If they are smaller than 3/8-inch (9mm) in diameter, use one part cement to one part stones, and no sand. If they are larger, use some sand in the mix: for example, one part cement, two parts sand, and three parts stones.

The topping layer must be thick enough to allow the stones to settle flush with the tops of the forms. Brush/flush as with the spreading method.

After curing, the exposed-ag surface can be brightened by a 1:10 muriatic acid/water wash, followed by a thorough rinse. A continual "wet" look is provided by coating the *dry* slab with a clear acrylic finish intended for outdoor use on concrete. Recommended are *Lustaglas* (Coatings Unlimited, Southern Pines, N.C. 28387); *Terra-Seal* (Hilliard Chemical Co., Box 909, St. Joseph, Mo. 64501); *EA Sealer* (Preco Chemical Corp., 55 Skyline Dr., Plainview, N.Y. 11803); and *Horntraz* (Dewey and Almy Chemical Div., 62 Whittemore Ave., Cambridge, Mass. 02140). These are also fine for coating brick-, stone-, and block-paved patios.

An interesting pockmarked texture can be added to your patio by sprinkling rock salt over its surface just before floating. Hand floating embeds the salt particles in the surface, to be washed out later to leave small holes. This finish is not recommended for freezing climates.

To make exposed aggregate by the spreading method, place the stones over the top of the slab while it's still soft and tap them in with 2 × 4 or wood float. Keep going until they're level with the surface. Expose them later.

TEXTURED CONCRETE

Magnesium float used after wood-floating produces a gritty-textured surface that's ideal for patios. This one incorporated a brown dust-on coloring that was sprinkled on and floated in during finishing.

Sponge-rubber float leaves the surface coarser than a magnesium float, still fine for a nonslip patio, though. Run the float over the surface in overlapping arcs after edging and jointing.

A stiff-bristled broom applied early makes for a coarse finish like this. For a finer texture, wait until the surface sets harder or use a softer broom, or both.

Cement and Concrete Assn. of England

PATTERNED CONCRETE

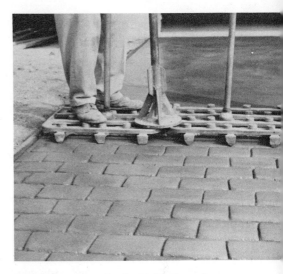

Pattern-stamped colored finish looks very much like brick, stone, tile — whatever it's patterned after. It's made by working patterning irons into the soft precolored surface.

Patterning tools are "walked in" to the surface after floating and initial troweling. Metal tamper (center) helps to embed them the required distance.

Slight tooling with a mason's jointing tool helps to clean up the lines of the pattern. If the project is small enough, the lines can be tooled in by hand.

Ends of the pattern are finished out with hand wedges to complete it across the slab. Most often, the dust-on coloring method is used to get color into the slab surface.

Portland Cement Assn.

Organic concrete stains can make a varicolored flagstone effect when the "flags" are tooled into the slab before it sets. Later the colors are brushed onto the flags. Final step is to stain the in-between joints.

What's called a travertine finish is easily made by casting a whipped-cream-thick slurry of white portland cement, a little coloring to produce an off-whitish color, and water over the floated slab. Use your hand or a wallpaper-paste brush. Let the topping stiffen slightly, then smooth down the high spots with a light pass of a steel trowel, leaving the depressions. This treatment is not recommended for freezing climates.

Real-looking imitation brick, tile, and stone patterns are made by impressing the soft, colored surface of the slab with special pattern-stamping tools. You'll either have to rent the tools, or make some yourself from metal. Or, you can score the surface with a groover or other tool in the desired pattern, but this takes more time. The best time to do it is immediately after the first floating and troweling, before too much stiffness sets in (see photos).

The bottoms of cans may be used to create circular patterns in fresh concrete. The edge or side of the trowel can make patterns. So can cookie cutters. Anything that pleases you can be pattern-stamped into your slab to give it an individualized texture.

Combination of Methods. Many of the best face-finishing methods may be used together for unusually beautiful results. For example, exposed-aggregate is often combined with plain trowel-finished concrete for decoration. Bricks may be worked into the surface to design or delineate. Brooming may be done in conjunction with a colored finish that is later pattern-stamped.

Whatever looks good to you is what you should try. Section the patio off into squares of perhaps four feet and tackle one square at a time. Just one an evening every day gets you big results within a month.

ESTIMATING VOLUME

SLAB THICKNESS	AREA (square feet)				AREA (square meters)			
	50	100	300	500	1	5	25	50
	CUBIC YARDS NEEDED (10% waste)				CUBIC YARDS NEEDED (10% waste)			
1½" (40mm)	¼	½	1½	2½	0.04	0.2	1	2
2" (50mm)	⅓	⅔	2	3½	0.06	0.3	1.4	2.8
3" (75mm)	½	1	3	5	0.08	0.4	2.0	4.1
4" (90mm)	⅔	1⅓	4	6¾	0.10	0.5	2.5	5.0

ESTIMATING MATERIALS

	MIX A: Use for 3″ (75mm) and thicker. Gives 1:2¼:3 propor.				MIX B: Stronger. Use for thin-section slabs. Gives 1:2:2¼ propor.			
	PORTLAND CEMENT	DAMP SAND	STONES (1″ max.)	YIELD (approx.)	PORTLAND CEMENT	DAMP SAND	STONES (¾″ max.)	YIELD (approx.)
PROPORTION (by volume)	1	2¼	3	3¼	1	2	2¼	3⅓
PER BAG OF CEMENT*	1 bag (50 kg.)	2½ cu. ft. ($0.07m^3$)	3⅓ cu. ft. ($0.09m^3$)	4⅓ cu. ft. ($0.40m^3$)	1 bag (50 kg.)	2¼ cu. ft. ($0.06m^3$)	2½ cu. ft. ($0.07m^3$)	3½ cu. ft. ($0.10m^3$)
PER CU. YD. OF CONCRETE*	6¼ bags (587½ lb.)	15.5 cu. ft. (1400 lb.)	21 cu. ft. (2100 lb.)	1 cu. yd.	7¾ (728½ lb.)	17 cu. ft. (1550 lb.)	19½ cu. ft. (1950 lb.)	1 cu. yd.
PER M^3 OF CONCRETE*	8¼ bags (352½ kg.)	$0.4m^3$	$0.6m^3$	$1m^3$	10 bags (427 kg.)	$0.5m^3$	$0.6m^3$	$1m^3$

* For 80-pound Canadian bags, multiply cement figures by 1.18

TABLE OF MIXES (parts by volume)

	PORTLAND CEMENT	DAMP SAND	STONES	WATER (first try)
MIX A	1	2¼	3 (1″ max. size) (25mm)	½
MIX B	1	2	2¼ (¾″ max. size) (20mm)	½

7 | Inexpensive Paving: Soil-Cement

MOST THINGS YOU'D BUY to build a patio have gone up in price recently. One hasn't: soil-cement. It's still dirt cheap. "Dirt-cement," as those who are very familiar with it lovingly call the material, contains a little portland cement — the same kind you use to make concrete — and a lot of good old *terra firma*. The dirt is free. The cement costs more than it did years ago, but it's still a bargain building material.

Soil-cement sets up hard, not as hard as concrete but hard enough to stabilize the soil completely. It makes an excellent patio paving at about a quarter the cost of ready-mixed concrete.

Soil-cement makes as great a subbase for a concrete patio as it does a finished paving material on its own. Soil-cement gets your outdoor living out of the mud without forcing you to haul in sand and stones. Besides, soil-cement is mostly your own native soil, blending in rather than contrasting with its surroundings.

One caution: don't expect a perfect pool-table-flat surface on your S/C patio. As best you build it, the surface will have irregularities, unless you're willing to build forms and strike it off like concrete. We don't recommend going to all that trouble.

How long will a soil-cement patio last? No one knows. The first engineered soil-cement road was built in 1935 using crude methods by today's standards, yet it's still in great shape. Some of the early soil-cement dams are still going strong, too. So it's no new thing.

Recently, retired professional engineer Franklin W. "Doc" Vaughan, a long-time soil-cement man who was involved in that first S/C road project, offered his expert advice on the subject. Through the years, he adapted his engineered soil-cement construction methods to home use with complete success.

"Anyone can make soil-cement at home," says Doc, "if they go about it right."

Here are the details of his procedure, including thicknesses and amounts of cement to use with various soil types. No sophisticated professional construction methods are required — nothing that you cannot bring to bear in your own backyard.

COST. The cost of soil-cement for a patio depends on how much portland cement you have to mix in with the soil to make it harden sufficiently. And that, in turn, depends on how well your soil and the cement react together.

Some soils — especially sandy or gravelly ones — can be hardened with just a little cement. Others, those containing lots of minute silt-sized particles, or those with organic matter, need more cement to make them harden. A little clay can be handled by using more cement. Dark-colored topsoils and soils containing much clay are unsuitable for soil-cement. If you have this type, you must dig them down to something more suitable or else haul in a better-reacting soil. Then you're getting to the work and expense of concrete.

The amount of portland cement needed to make soil-cement runs from a low of six percent to a high of 16 percent cement, by volume.

SIMPLIFIED MIX PROPORTIONS

SOIL TYPE	ADD CEMENT
Average sand-clay (sand with a little clay for binder)	10%
Appreciable clay	12%
Sandy soil, budget job, take a chance	8½-9%

GETTING STARTED. Begin your S/C-patio paving project like any other, by removing the grass and topsoil in the area to be paved. Decide on the depth to be stabilized. Doc Vaughan recommends five inches for a patio, while admitting that he's seen successful ones built as thin as three inches. If your climate is a rough one for ground freezing and thawing, better make yours six inches deep to be sure.

Next decide on the percentage of portland cement to be used. The table below tells you how much. Try to avoid using "heavy" or stiff clay-like soils since they take lots of cement and are hard to pulverize and mix with the cement.

Spreading. With your ground prepared, spread the cement out over it. The easiest way to gauge an accurate cement-spread is to scratch the patio off into grids of the size called for in the table. You may vary their dimensions—keeping the net area the same—to suit the patio's dimensions. It's best to keep your grids as close to square as possible.

For example, to get a 10-percent cement content in a 5-inch-deep pavement, according to the table, you'd need one standard 94-pound bag of portland cement for every 24 square feet. Grids 4 by 6 feet thus get one bag of cement each.

If the project were a 20 by 27-foot patio, you could mark out 20 4 by 6-foot grids on it, as shown in the drawing, with five half-grids left over along one edge. Each full grid would get one bag of cement. Each half grid would get a half bag. For the total job, you'd need 23 bags, with half a bag left over.

HOW MUCH CEMENT YOU NEED (94-lb., 1-cu.-ft. bags)

ONE BAG COVERS*

SOIL TYPE	CEMENT	INCHES/FEET			METRIC		
		4″ Deep	5″ Deep	6″ Deep	100mm Deep	125mm Deep	150mm Deep
Sandy and gravelly	10%	30 sq. ft. (5′ × 6′ grid)	24 sq. ft. (4′ × 6′ grid)	20 sq. ft. (4′ × 5′ grid)	2.8m² (1.4 × 2.0m grid)	2.2m² (1.4 × 2.0m grid)	1.9m² (1.2 × 1.6m grid
Containing much clay	12%	25 sq. ft. (5′ × 5′ grid)	20 sq. ft. (4′ × 5′ grid)	16 sq. ft. (4′ × 4′ grid)	2.3m² (1.2 × 1.9m grid)	1.9m² (1.2 × 1.6m grid)	1.5m² (1.0 × 1.5m grid)
Containing much clay plus frost-protection	14%	20 sq. ft. (4′ × 5′ grid)	16 sq. ft. (4′ × 4′ grid)	12 sq. ft. (3′ × 4′ grid)	1.9m² (1.2 × 1.6m grid)	1.5m² (1.0 × 1.5m grid)	1.1m² (1.0 × 1.1m grid)
Budget mixture with good-acting soil only	8½-9%	33 sq. ft. (5½′ × 6′ grid)	26 sq. ft. (5′2½″ × 5′ grid)	22 sq. ft. (5½′ × 4′ grid)	3.0m² (1.5 × 2.0m grid)	2.4m² (4.0 × 6.0m grid)	2.0m² (4.0 × 5.0m grid)

* For 80-lb. Canadian bag multiply sq. ft. figures by 0.85

Mark your patio off into grids, according to those in the table on page 93. Put one sack of cement in the center of each grid, open it and spread the cement evenly over the entire grid.

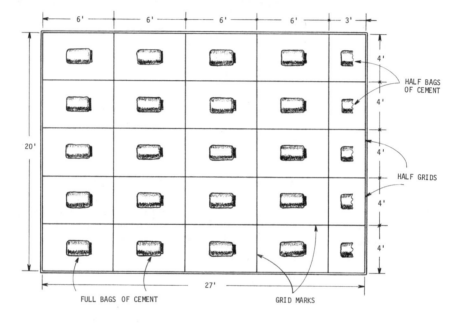

HALF BAGS
OF CEMENT

HALF GRIDS

FULL BAGS OF CEMENT

GRID MARKS

CEMENT SPREAD

The easiest way to open bags of cement quickly is to slash one end open with a shovel, then lift the bag, letting its cement pour out. Once this is done, you must complete all the other steps in the soil-cement process without stopping.

Better than mixing by hand is to use a roto-tiller. It does the job quickly with the least effort.
You can rent one — any size will do.

Set the tiller's depth spike to make the tines cut
and mix to the desired depth. It takes only
about two passes of the roto-tiller to get a uniform blend.

Spread only as much cement as you can work at a single stretch without stopping,
even for a coffee break. Once the cement contacts damp earth, it begins setting.
Thus, once you start, you have to keep going right through to the last step.

Open each sack, dump it, and rake the cement out over its grid. An even depth is
what you're after.

Mixing. If there is much area to do, rent or buy a roto-tiller, because mixing is the
toughest part of the job. Small jobs may be mixed with a shovel, rake, hoe, or whatever is at hand.

Small rocks should be mixed right in. They're no trouble. Big rocks make it difficult to get a good blend of soil and cement, so they should be taken out as you en-
counter them. Mix to your chosen depth as closely as you can. If you mix too deep,
you get a thicker — but weaker — soil-cement layer. If you mix too shallow, you get a
stronger layer, but a too-thin one. With a roto-tiller, it's easy to go too deep.

Shovel test checks mix depth and
uniformity. To make it, dig several
holes around the patio and measure down to the color-change line
for depth. Check the diggings for
an even color, indicating the soil-
cement has been well blended.

Use what's called the "shovel test" to check for mix depth and uniformity (see photo). When you're at the right depth and the mix is well blended, you're ready for the next step.

Adding water. At this point, the soil-cement will be dry and dusty; the cement dries up any water in the soil. To provide enough water to harden the cement, and for good compaction later on, you'll have to add some and mix again. Spray the water on with a garden-hose spray, making the coverage as even as possible. Don't add so much water at one time that it washes the soil. After each water application, mix once more to full depth. Use the hand-squeeze test to tell when the water content is right (see photo).

Rake out the surface smoothly after the last mixing. Compaction can now begin. Do it with a home-built hand-tamper. Use a 6-foot-long 4 × 4 with an 8-inch square of plywood nailed to one end, or a flat 2 × 10 with a pair of 1 × 2 handles nailed to the sides. If there's much area to do, you can rent a power tamper.

If you can get your car onto the patio, run its tires back and forth over the hand-tamped surface to compact it further. However you do it, the initial compaction should leave the soil-cement firm and dense all over.

The surface may be uneven because some spots will compact more than others. To remedy this, scratch the surface all over with the tines of a rake to loosen up some soil-cement. Grade this loose material out smoothly with a board and hand-tamp once more. During this final compaction, moisten the surface *slightly* with a fine spray from the hose nozzle.

Curing. Now it's all done but the curing. Like concrete, soil-cement needs several days or a week of damp-curing. Keep it damp by sprinkling with water. Don't let the surface dry out during the whole time. Sprinkle lightly the first day because the soil-cement mixture still has not hardened much. It's okay to walk on it, however, if you don't mind leaving foot marks in the finished job. After the first day, you can sprinkle as hard as you like without hurting the soil-cement — it is on its way to becoming impervious to water. Even a rain, except for the worst gully-washer coming right after final compaction, shouldn't hurt it unless the slab is undermined in a washout. Even then, the soil-cement probably wouldn't be affected. I've seen sections of soil-cement roads that were completely tunneled under by water, yet carried traffic without a stop. The soil-cement formed a short, effective bridge.

Surfacing. Roads and streets made of soil-cement get what's called a "bituminous-surface treatment" to keep traffic from wearing the surface away. Whether or not you'll put such a finish on your project depends on your climate as well as on your preference. The surfacing helps soil-cement to take severe weathering. It hides the natural dirt-like appearance of soil-cement, so you may prefer to omit it. What you can do is wait and see what a winter's exposure does to your soil-cement, then decide whether to surface it or not. If there is any scaling or abrading, give it the protective topping, as follows:

Get a 5-gallon can of emulsified asphalt, the soupy kind used for installing cold-applied roll roofing. Johns-Manville call theirs Duplex Cement. For better penetration, thin the asphalt with solvent, the kind directed on the label. Adding 1/4-part thinner usually does the job. Brush the black mixture liberally over the surface of your cured and cleaned soil-cement patio. Before it dries, cast a thin layer of fine sand onto the asphalt. Asphalt will bind the sand particles into a thin layer adhering to the soil-cement. Until dry, don't walk on it or you might track black asphalt into the house. When completely dry, sweep off the excess sand.

Sprinkle water over the mixed soil-cement. Try to get even coverage without washing the soil.

Mix to blend in the water full depth. One pass with the tiller usually does it. It may take several sprinklings followed by mixing to get sufficient water into the mix.

Hand-squeeze test tells when the water content is correct. When you can squeeze a soil sample into a lump in your hand, then break it in two without crumbling, the moisture content is perfect.

Compact your soil-cement with a hand tamper. Pack it down as tightly as it will go. The tighter you compact, the harder the soil-cement will become.

If possible, use your car to roll down the surface. Drive over every part you can reach. Hand-tamp those that you cannot. Rolling is a good follow-up to an initial hand-tamping.

Scratch the surface with a rake and use the loosenings to smooth out unevenness. Hand-tamp to compact the top layer, then you can relax — your soil-cement is finished.

Cure by keeping the surface continually damp for several days, longer in cool weather. Don't expect a surface as smooth as concrete. Remember that 90 percent of it is dirt.

TIPS ON DOING IT. That's the soil-cement process. Here are a few additional tips that may help:

• Be sure to use only Type 1 or Type 2 portland cement. Don't use plastic or mortar cement, or concrete mixes.

• If you have any doubt about what type of soil you have, test it with cement. That's what the engineers do. Make small samples, parceling out the various volumes with a kitchen measuring cup. For example, one measuring cup of cement mixed with ten cups of your soil gives a 10-percent mixture by volume. (Note: proportions of cement by volume are figured as *added to* the given volume of soil.) To get a 12-percent mixture, mix one cup of cement with 8⅓ cups of soil. For a 14-percent mixture, mix one cup of cement with 7⅛ cups of soil (approx.). An ultimately strong 16-percent mixture is made by adding one cup of cement to 6¼ cups of soil. And for a "budget mixture," try mixing one cup of cement with 11 or even 12 parts of a good-acting soil.

Make up a whole range of samples. Mix them to the degree you'll be willing to mix when in place on the patio. Add water to satisfy the squeeze-test, mix again. Then compact each one into a tin can or wood mold. Label and keep the samples damp for a week. Then check on their hardness. Remember that dark-colored soils contain decomposed organic matter that can slow down the setting of soil-cement. Let them harden much longer.

A test sample of soil-cement — made with ample cement mixed with soil and tamped into an empty can — makes a ringing sound when the can is peeled away ten days later.

You can use soil-cement for setting fence posts around your patio. Add about 20 percent cement to the diggings (even black dirt will harden with that much cement), mix (adding water), then compact the S/C back into the hole around the post. It will be held solidly.

If any sample doesn't get hard, it contains too little cement. Tap each sample with a hammer. Properly hard, it should produce a ringing sound. Once you've found the right amount of cement for your soil, you can size your cement-spreads from the table with complete confidence.

- Cool weather is best for making soil-cement. It stays workable longer. Don't try soil-cementing in freezing weather, though.

- If your patio is too big to tackle at one session, divide it into sections. Do first one section, then another. Finish one before starting the next. When you mix a new section next to an old one, be sure to carry the blending operation about an inch into the older section. This helps tie the two sections together.

- There is no need to edge a soil-cement patio unless you want to. Soil-cement serves as its own edging.

- You may notice tiny cracks developing as moisture leaves the soil-cement. Clay soils will shrink more than sandy or gravelly ones. This is normal. The cracks will do it no harm.

- To use S/C for a subbase beneath a concrete or paver patio, a leaner mixture will do. One containing about half the normal amount of cement usually suffices to toughen the soil. The engineers call this a cement-treated subbase. It won't wash out, and it stays put.

8 | Cast Your Patio Indoors, Tote It Out

PRECASTING PATIO TILES is one way to make a great-looking patio. This method lets you take things in nice, easy stages. Night or day, rain or shine, you can cast one tile or a dozen at a time. Do it in your basement or garage if you like. Start in winter, and by spring you'll have enough units completed to lay the whole patio.

An easy method that we developed uses palletized construction. Fresh tiles are built and handled on pieces of plywood until they've set enough to make it alone. Since the tiles are only 1½ inches (40mm) thick, the colorful exposed-aggregate tiles will make for a lower cost patio than if you built it 4-inches thick of ordinary gray concrete.

You can make your tiles square, rectangular, round or in some special shape, like the Mediterranean motif shown. Any form that leaves no fragile projections to be broken off will work. Give some thought to how the tiles will fit together to make up the whole patio, also to the weight of the tiles. A limit of about 50 pounds per tile is reasonable. This was about what ours weighed. Whatever the shape, plan on using pea gravel, or on growing grass between the tiles.

MAKING THE FORM. Build the form first. One form is all you need because it is stripped after casting a tile and set up right away for the next one.

Our tile pattern makes good use of a 2 by 2-foot plywood casting-carrying pallet. Its Mediterranean motif can be cut from one length of 2 × 8 lumber 60 inches long without waste. First cut the 2 × 8 exactly in half. Next, saber-saw semicircular cuts centered in each half to make the rounded-out portions. The cutouts are then sliced in two and the four quarter "pies" nailed back on the 2 × 8 with their curved sides out (see drawing).

The forms are held at the ends by 1 × 2s slipped over assembly pins made from nails with the heads nipped off. Right-angled curtain-rod hangers placed in the form just beyond the ends of each 1 × 2 are turned to hold the 1 × 2s in. Turned the other way, they release. This lets you take the form apart for reuse. Before using the form each day, oil it with nondetergent motor oil, then it will part cleanly from the tile. Key marks on the form's parts speed assembly.

During casting, the 2 by 2-foot plywood pallets serve as the bottom of the form. Cleats nailed to the form hold it in position over the pallets. Have a pallet for each tile you plan to build at each precasting session. By the next go-round, the first set of tiles should be strong enough to slide off their pallets. In any case, give them at least three days. Then the pallets can be used again. One 4 × 8 sheet of ¾-inch exterior C-C (or better) plugged and touch-sanded plywood provides eight pallets, about all you'll need.

A full sheet of ¾-inch plywood nailed across two sawhorses makes a nice working platform. Both form and pallet are clamped to the top of this work table with C-

By precasting the tiles, you can built a striking terrazzo patio for less money than you'd spend on a plain gray one. Using tiles lets you precast indoors, set tiles outdoors later.

Forms for our Mediterranean motif tiles (left) are made from a pair of 30" 2 × 8s. The 6½" radius semicircles are cut out with a saber saw, then sawed in half and attached to the ends of the 2 × 8s with corrugated fasteners.

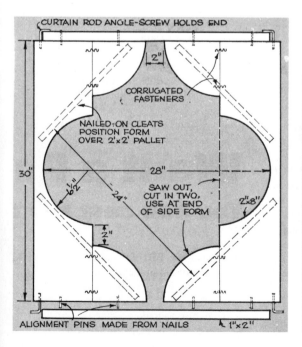

CURTAIN ROD ANGLE-SCREW HOLDS END

2"

CORRUGATED FASTENERS

NAILED-ON CLEATS POSITION FORM OVER 2'x2' PALLET

28"

SAW OUT, CUT IN TWO, USE AT END OF SIDE FORM

30"

6½"

24"

2"x8"

2"

ALIGNMENT PINS MADE FROM NAILS

1"x2"

clamps or large-capacity spring clamps. To save oiling the pallets, lay a polyethylene bond-breaker sheet between the form and pallet. If you want smooth tile surfaces, be sure the sheet lies flat. Wrinkles will imprint onto the surface.

TERRAZZO COURSE. Tiles are cast with the two-course method. No need for a bonding agent, as in a two-course cast-in-place patio, because the second course is placed while the first is still plastic. Since tiles are cast upside down, the top terrazzo course goes into the form first. Make it with white portland cement, a concrete-coloring pigment, and 3/8-inch or smaller marble chips. Making colored concrete is described in the chapter on concrete-patio construction.

You have some decisions to make before you can buy the materials: color of the concrete background matrix, and color of the terrazzo chips. The matrix may be of any color: pure white (not recommended because it's too bright), or any of those named in the chapter on casting a concrete patio. The amount of coloring pigment may be as little as 1½ percent to as high as 10 percent by weight of cement — never more. Weigh-batch both the cement and the coloring pigment for uniformity of color. For example, to make a 7-percent colored mix, dump one pound (0.45 kg) of pigment into 14 pounds (6.4 kg) of cement. For a 1½-percent colored mix, put four ounces (0.11 kg) of coloring pigment weighed on a postal scale, into 16½ pounds (7.5 kg) of cement. Dry-mix cement and pigment thoroughly.

White cement, coloring pigments and marble chips all can be found at terrazzo-supply houses. See the yellow pages of your telephone directory. Concrete-products suppliers often carry these materials, too.

The materials batched out for one tile are shown, base course on the left and terrazzo course on the right. Batch cans ensure correct proportions, batch to batch. Water is batched in cut-off half-gallon milk cartons. Pails fit small mixer (right).

Small-batch concrete mixer sold by Montgomery Ward uses a 5-gallon pail as its mixing drum. It's perfect for a tile-precasting project. One drum can be mixing while you're preparing ingredients for the next batch.

Real terrazzo contains marble chips because marble grinds easily. You won't be grinding your tiles, and so you can use any weather-resistant stone or ceramic chips that go well with the matrix color you've chosen. Sometimes two different colors of chips are blended for effect. Two sizes, too. But to keep the beauty layer thin, chips should be no larger than ⅜ inch. Smaller ¼-inch ones would be preferable. Chips are normally sold in 100-pound bags.

It's a good idea to make a test sample of your terrazzo mix before going ahead. After hardening, quick-dry the sample in a warm oven to get an idea of what the finished patio tile will look like.

TOPPING COURSE. To begin precasting tiles, you'll need some empty cans for batching and mixing of materials. Later you'll need a wire brush for exposing the pretty stone chips. In any case, get about 100 square feet of smooth 6-mil polyethylene plastic sheeting for use in casting and curing tiles. A small pointed rectangular trowel is useful for handling and spreading mixes. It's not essential, though.

Either buy a small five-gallon-pail concrete mixer (Montgomery Ward is the only place I know to get them) or do your mixing by hand with a hoe and mortar box. In any case, mix one part precolored portland cement, one part stone chips, and about one-half part water (by volume). If you use our tile design, you can apply the quantities shown in the table. Otherwise you'll have to juggle your proportions to come out with the right amount of mix for casting one tile.

When thoroughly blended for about a minute, the terrazzo course can be dumped into the form. Spread it evenly over the form bottom with a small trowel. To save on hand-spreading, you can make a vibrating table (see photo). Simply mount an old ¼- or ⅓-hp. electric motor with eccentric weight to the table. When you turn the motor

Terrazzo pour starts with the form firmly clamped to the work table. Plywood pallet and plastic bond-breaker sheet are beneath the form. Spread the terrazzo mix with a small trowel to cover the entire form. Then turn on the vibrator.

Vibrator can be made from an old washing-machine motor. Lead weight was cast in a 1½" pipe, bored off-center for the motor shaft, and tapped for a set-screw to hold it on. For safety, the vibrator should be covered with a pail while it runs.

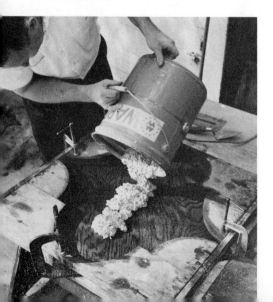

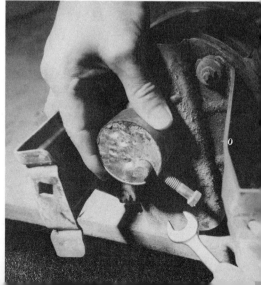

on, the table will jiggle rapidly and your terrazzo course will "melt" into place. Without the vibrating table, you'll have to hammer the work table surface about 20 times around the outside of the form. Either way, stop the vibration as soon as "soup" starts running out beneath the form.

The Terrazzo layer shouldn't be much thicker than a single layer of chips.

BASE COURSE. Follow immediately with the plain gray concrete base course. You can make it with ready-packaged sand-mix (also called *topping*) or by proportioning the ingredients from a sack of portland cement and a pile of sand. If you mix your own base course, use one part cement and three parts damp, loose concrete sand. Mix dry, then add the required water. So you can strip the form right away, it's important to go easy on water. You want a stiff mix that will stand by itself, not run into a mushy pile. Try this test: Squeeze your mix into a tight ball in your hand. If you can do it without getting your fingers very wet, it's okay. If the sand you use is already damp, not much water will have to be added. A stiff mix gives another important advantage besides fast form removal — strength.

Mix only enough base course to fill the form. Placed into the form and vibrated, the fresh terrazzo and base courses will bond together as though they were one piece.

If your mix was properly stiff, the form can be carefully stripped right away. A little edge-slumping will not show on the surface of the tile. On the Mediterranean tile, it pays to break the form bond first at the curve, not at the point.

Form off, pick up the plywood pallet with the face grain running *across* between your hands; it bends least when held this way. Carry it off to where the tile can cure undisturbed. After doing a few tiles, the precasting process becomes almost automatic.

Stiff, dry base-course concrete is placed over the vibrated terrazzo course while still wet. Spread it gently to prevent punch-through to the surface of the tile. Vibrating helps. Base contains cement and sand, no stones.

Smooth out the base course across the forms with a float and vibrate before leaving it. The finish needn't be pretty, just reasonably even. It will be the bottom of the tile when placed in the patio. Top will be the terrazzo course.

Slice all around the form with an old table knife to separate it from the tile. This step minimizes edge-tearing when you remove the form. If the concrete was properly stiff, the forms can then be removed without waiting for the concrete to set.

Disassemble the form's parts and gently lift them away from the fresh tile. Although this tile was only a few minutes old, note how well its stiff concrete holds shape without the form. Some edge-slumping is okay, since most of it occurs at the bottom of the tile.

If you mix both terrazzo and base courses in the same container, be sure to rinse it well after doing a base course. Otherwise the darker base-course mix will discolor the next terrazzo mix. You needn't rinse before mixing base course.

If you use the Wards mixer, it pays to have an extra five-gallon pail so you can batch out one course while the other is mixing. With this kind of production, you'll be turning out three tiles an hour by yourself in no time. A helper can double that rate.

TERRAZZO EXPOSURE. Keep checking on your first-made tiles. When their bottoms have set to a dried-mud hardness, they're ready for aggregate-exposure. To do this, you'll need to turn each one over. No problem, just lay an empty pallet over the bottom of the tile, sandwiching the tile between the two pallets. Squeeze gently, lift and invert. Don't drop the sandwich or the fresh tile is a goner. Once flipped, the pallet and bond-breaker sheet lift off to expose the smooth-textured top surface.

Abrade just enough colored-matrix mortar from the surface with a wire brush to expose the tops of the terrazzo chips. This opens their color to view.

With most terrazzo mixes, brushing is best done eight to 10 hours after casting. Beyond that time, the surface becomes too hard to brush easily. You can brush nicely at just six hours, but handling tiles that soon is tricky.

If you must wait beyond 10 hours to brush, the game is not lost. Chuck a tungsten-carbide-impregnated sanding disk in the disk-sander attachment of your electric drill and go over the tile's surface. Chips are exposed even neater than brushing. You may even prefer to wait and disk-sand rather than wire-brush because it offers more leeway in timing of the operation. It adds disks to the cost, though. The ideal disking time is about 12 to 15 hours, which means evening casting and next-morning brushing.

Using either the wire-brush or disk method, you can expose about six tiles an hour. Stack the finished tiles out of the way for curing.

To invert the 8- to 10-hour-old tiles for surface brushing that exposes their attractive stone chips, sandwich them between two pallets. Squeeze as you gently turn them over, face up. Pallet and plastic sheet will lift off.

Wire-brush the tile's surface just enough to remove mortar from the colorful stone chips. Timing of this step is important, allowing only a couple of hours' leeway. If you wait too long, brushing will be difficult.

ACID-CLEANING. After curing but before laying tiles, etch-clean their faces with a 1:10 solution of muriatic acid and water. This removes any cement stains from the chips, leaving them clear and bright. Brush on the acid solution, let it stop bubbling, then flood with water from a garden hose. If any of the chips contain calcium — limestone and marble do — don't wait for the bubbling to stop — rinse right away. On the other hand, granite, quartz, feldspar, and silica aggregates aren't harmed by a long acid-etch.

Disc-sanding the tiles will work when they're too hard for wire-brushing. For best results, use a tungsten-carbide-impregnated metal sanding disc in your electric-drill attachment. One disc will do about fifteen tiles before it wears out.

Lay a large plastic sheet over the finished tiles to damp-cure them. Curing should continue for at least six days after casting the last one. Tiles may be stacked up to six deep with one day of setting between each layer.

Let the tiles dry thoroughly, then coat them with a clear concrete sealer, brushed or rolled on. (See the chapter on building a concrete patio for a list of good clear sealers.) Apply the sealer according to directions on the container.

LAYING TILES. Lay the tiles out in sand as described in the chapter on building a paver patio. The tiles may be butted tightly or spaced apart. We spaced ours two inches and filled the joints with dark gravel for contrast.

Protect the appearance of your one-of-a-kind patio by hosing it clean when dirt collects. The clear sealer may need occasional renewal.

QUANTITIES. To tell how many tiles you'll need, divide the area of your patio in square feet by the number of square feet in a single tile. Our tiles contain three square feet each (0.3 m²).

To make each tile, you'll need the following quantities of materials. To order materials, multiply by the number of tiles you'll be making:

> White cement — 4.5 pounds (2 kg)
> Marble chips — 5.5 pounds (2.5 kg)
> Color pigment —
>   @ 7 percent — 4.8 ounces (136 gm)
>   @ 1½ percent — 1 ounce (28 gm)
> Regular cement — 9 pounds (4 kg)
> Concrete sand — 36 pounds (16.4 kg)

Lay your cured tiles out on the tamped, dampened sand bedding. A stretched string and some spacer blocks will help you to get straight rows and even joints. Tiles of this pattern interlock to form a continuous surface with gaps only around the edges. Gaps are later filled by pieces of tiles.

If you cut pieces rather than form them, chisel a line along the cut, then jump on both halves of the tile with the cut line laid over a steel rod. Plywood strips on either side of the rod catch the pieces and prevent points of the pattern from breaking off.

Fill the spaced joints, if you wish, by raking contrasting gravel into them. Redwood strips (2″ × 2″) staked along the edges hold the tiles together and keep them from spreading. They are held to the ground with steel stakes.

Precast concrete pavers can be made in rectangles and squares. Side dimensions are in multiples of 1, 2, and 3 to make everything fit together. Draw your pattern out on squared paper and make the required number of each.

In place of regular cement and concrete sand, you may use 45 pounds (20.5 kg) of prepackaged sand-mix concrete.

These figures are for a 3-foot-square tile. To convert to other tile sizes, simply divide each by three on your pocket calculator and multiply by the square-foot size of one of your tiles.

Hexagons make an excellent interlocking pattern. Here the edges are not finished off with pieces, but left zig-zag. A few darker-colored tiles here and there add accent. No exposed-aggregate effect was used.

It's tough to beat grass as a between-tile treatment. To get it, fill the joints with good soil, then plant and fertilize just as you would a lawn. Don't forget to water lightly during hot, dry weather.

9 | Other Patio/Deck Building Materials

WOOD AND CONCRETE make patios and decks, but so do lots of other materials. Don't restrict your thinking to only the well-knowns. Here are some different materials, with a brief how-to given for each.

Asphalt. You can lay an asphalt patio that, with maintenance, will last as long as a concrete one. The dark color may or may not be an advantage, depending on how much sun the patio gets. Asphalt's blackness makes the patio low on reflected glare but high on absorbed heat. It's unsuitable for around a swimming pool or other sunny spot, but okay for shady locations.

You can use asphalt by itself or side by side with other paving types. The easiest way to get it is to call an asphalt contractor, but that's not cheap. You can do it yourself if you're careful to get the asphalt sloped properly and without low spots called "birdbaths."

Use "cold-mix" asphalt. Cold-mix may be purchased in sacks at your building materials dealer. It's also used for patching.

Make a good 2-inch-thick subbase of sand to separate the asphalt from wet or cracking soil. If your soil is sandy and well drained, you won't need a special subbase. At any rate, slope the patio $1/8$ to $1/4$ inch per foot away from the house for drainage.

Install edging boards as in forming for a concrete patio. However, light lumber, such as 1 × 2s, may be used in place of heavier concrete-forming lumber. Use redwood, cypress or pressure-treated wood if you want a lasting job.

Dump out the cold-mix over the area to be paved, spacing the dump piles about a foot apart. Then spread the mounds out level with a garden rake. The mixture should end up about two inches thick.

The cold-mix smooth, you can compact it. If you have much area to work, rent a power tamper or power-driven roller. Otherwise, a heavy garden roller—the heavier the better—will work. Wet the roller surface with water so asphalt won't stick to it. Roll until the roller leaves no edges as it passes.

If you want a lighter color, sprinkle sand or fine, white stone chips over the surface, rolling them in. Crushed brick works well, too. The patio is ready to use as soon as you finish rolling. Certain floor and deck paints can be used to color an asphalt patio. See a paint dealer.

Loose paving. You can cover nontrafficked areas of your patio with loose paving materials such as stones, crushed brick, wood chips, bark, sawdust, or decomposed granite. These are often used around patio paving to save paving areas where you won't be walking much.

To make them, install 1 × 2 edging as for asphalt paving. Spread and rake out the materials within the edging. You needn't worry about sloping or creating birdbaths because the materials are porous and will drain naturally. For this reason loose mate-

Jim Walter Corp.

Chips for loose ground cover come in four sizes of white crystalline Georgia marble. You simply spread, and rake smooth. Bagged chips are sold in 50-pound sacks from garden stores, chain stores and stone yards.

Flagstones are considered by some to be the ultimate in patio quality. They may be set mortarless on sand or on a concrete slab in mortar and with their joints mortared.

Weathered effect of flagstones adds to patio beauty. Straight edges on the outer stones calls for careful cutting or sawing with an abrasive blade in a power saw. You can try doing it or ask your stone dealer to do the trimming for you.

Broken pieces of stone, which sell at considerably less per pound than prime flags, make a stone-covered patio at a price. These stone pieces measure some six inches on a side.

rials are often placed around trees so the roots can get water and breathe. If you want to avoid the problem of weeds growing through, lay the loose materials on top of a sheet of 6-mil black polyethylene.

Maintenance of loose materials isn't easy. Raking will pretty well remove twigs and sticks, but not decayed leaves and dirt. When the loose fill gets dirty, you may have to dig it out and replace it.

Adobe blocks. If you live in a warm, dry climate and want an earthy looking paving for a patio, look at adobe blocks. They don't cost much and may be laid in sand-like no-mortar bricks (see Chapter 5). A life of ten years is not unusual. Avoid adobe if your annual rainfall is more than about 30 inches or if your ground freezes in winter. They won't take that.

Building-stone cutoffs left after a church job were used to make a rich-looking patio surface at moderate cost. Here they were laid tight together in mortar but without grouting the joints.

Rigid tile. No material makes a richer looking patio or deck than rigid tile. These can be quarry tile, slate, or ceramic mosaic tile. On concrete, you set them in mortar just as you lay bricks and stones. Joints are filled with plain or colored mortar after the base mortar has had time to cure hard. Final cleanup is with a brushed-on 1:10 muriatic acid/water solution, followed by rinsing. This removes mortar stains from the faces of the tiles. Wear goggles and either dipped or rubber gloves.

On a wood deck, the tiles can go on with what's called the thin-set method. The deck should be of exterior plywood stiff enough that it doesn't flex much between supports. Use the following span/thicknesses for Group 1 or Structural I plywood:

Span	Thickness
16″	$1/2''$
20″	$5/8''$
24″	$3/4''$, $7/8''$
32″	2-4-1, $1 1/4''$

Blocking must be used beneath unsupported joints in plywood panels, no different than for any plywood flooring or decking. Be sure to fill and smooth any cracks and joints in the concrete. The surface should be free of paint, oil, grease and the like.

Adhesive must be suitable for outdoor use. Generally, this limits you to the epoxy-type flooring adhesives. Spread the adhesive with a notched trowel having the notch configuration specified for the adhesive used. When the adhesive has dried properly, and before it sets too much, lay the tiles in it. When hard, grout and clean up as outlined above. Use flexible grout over a wood deck, regular grout over concrete. Grout is sand-mix concrete or "topping." If you cannot buy flexible floor grout, you can make it by adding one part white-vinyl concrete bonding agent to three parts of mix water in ordinary sand-mix concrete. The bonding agent lends flexibility to any grout made with it.

In mild, dry climates, adobe blocks make excellent paving. Set them on a smoothed subbase of sand or sandy soil. The 2 × 4 edging helps keep them from separating, once laid. Various sizes are available for a variety of patterns.

Nothing beats a quarry tile patio for elegance. This one was edged with polished marble. Quarry tiles need a solid concrete slab underneath. Tiles are set in mortar and their joints grouted.

Natural slate tiles are set in mortar on a concrete base for a high-class patio surface. Unless you have lots of money to spend, better restrict these architectural-type surfaces to small areas.

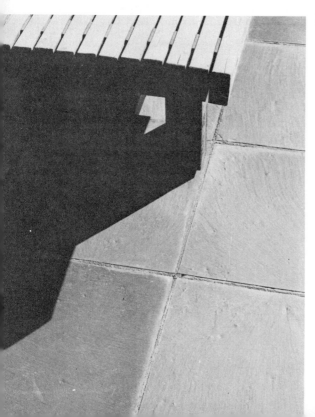

Unglazed ceramic tiles on concrete create a classy architectural look at somewhat less cost. Still, they're not cheap. You can buy them in ready-patterned 12"-by-12" sheets or get boxes of individual tiles and lay them one by one in epoxy-tube adhesive or mortar.

National Concrete Masonry Assn.

For a tiled effect at a low cost, use concrete blocks set in sand. Joints may be swept full of sand or left open. This kind of surface is laid like the one for a mortarless brick patio described in a previous chapter.

Quarry tiles can be laid on a plywood deck or concrete patio by running weatherproof construction adhesive on the backs, then setting them. A half-inch space between tiles allows later grouting with flexible grout, colored gray or black to hide soil.

Vinyl tile. You can choose from among many styles of vinyl tile that resemble brick, quarry tile, and stone without the effort or cost of these products. Even the feel and texture of tile matches the real thing.

Vinyl tiles may be installed on a concrete slab or a plywood deck (the same as above). Use an exterior type of adhesive, such as Kentile Epoxy Type No. 9. Spread it with a trowel having the epoxy notch configuration. Epoxy adhesive's coverage on concrete is about 250 sq. ft. per gallon. Temperature is important because heat sets the epoxy. Work only when the temperature is between 70 and 75° F., and don't work in direct sunlight.

Set tiles after 30 minutes but before 1½ hours. Roll or press each one firmly into place. Rolling is best. If you must step on the freshly tiled area, lay down plywood or boards. After 48 hours, you can hose down the job with complete assurance that it is weather-proof.

Carpeting. Either indoor/outdoor carpeting or one of the artificial turfs make a great patio surface. To lay carpet, clean and prepare the surface—plywood or concrete—as for vinyl-tiling. If you plan to place carpet over asphalt, first seal the asphalt with shellac to prevent bleeding.

Carpeted patio sunken to meet the half-basement floor level was covered with 3'-wide strips of Ozite Colony Point indoor/outdoor carpeting using the glue-down method (see text). Carpeting wraps up the sides to cover the entire enclosure. Stone chips surround it.

You have a choice of loose-laying carpeting like a rug, edge-fastening with double-faced tape, or full glue-down with adhesives.

To begin any of the methods, cut and lay out the pieces of carpeting side by side face up. If there are arrows on the back, these should all point in the same direction. Usually the edges of strips will butt together and make a tight seam. If they don't, turn the pieces over and snap chalk lines about half an inch in from the edges. Then cut the carpet along the chalk lines. Use a razor blade, knife, and straightedge. Turn the carpeting face up again with the arrows parallel. You're ready to complete the installation.

For a loose-lay job, roll out seam tape, such as Ozite's PT 201 stainless-steel locking-pin tape. Instructions come with the roll. This tape is used to hold the seams together and down.

In a perimeter installation, use either double-faced carpeting tape or an exterior carpet adhesive, such as Ozite's AP 900. Mark the surface of the patio or deck where the seams will come. Turn back the carpeting and place tape or spread adhesive along both sides of seam lines. Place one side of the seam down on the sticky stuff and carefully butt-join the second side to it. Do all the other seams the same way, including those along walls and at patio/deck edges.

For the best glued-down installation, turn back the edges of each piece of carpet and spread exterior-carpet adhesive (such as Ozite AP 400 or AP 770) two to three feet wide on both sides of the line. Butt the carpet edges as for the perimeter installation. Then turn back and spread for the rest of the carpet until all has been adhered. Press the carpet into the adhesive and work out any air pockets as you go. Use hand pressure or the back of a push-broom. If desired, edging materials can be used at doorways and around the perimeter.

Some kinds of carpet tiles may be bought in indoor/outdoor materials shops. A few of these are even self-stick. Outdoors, though, carpet tiles should be glued down with an outdoor adhesive whether they're self-sticking or not. Spread the adhesive and lay the tiles in it.

Wood with concrete. If you have access to rot-resistant wood and want to use it in combination with concrete or loose materials for your patio, this may be your way to go. The wood is often in the form of log rounds or railroad ties — new or used. If the wood is redwood or cypress, you needn't worry about rotting. But if it is another wood, you'd best soak it in preservative first. A simple soaking tank can be made by digging a hole in the ground large enough to hold the largest piece. Line the hole with polyethylene sheeting and pour in creosote or penta-type wood preservative. Submerge each piece of wood in preservative for a day. Lift it out, wearing dipped or rubber gloves. Stack to dry.

Set the wood pieces in place before you fill around them. Build up or dig out under them so their tops come level with the tops of the forms. For an exposed-ag effect, insert pebbles into the in-between concrete before it sets.

Pebble mosaics. You can make great-looking pebble mosaics using colorful, rounded beach stones. These may be purchased by the bag or collected from public lands along beaches and streams. (Before you collect on private land, be sure to ask the owner.) Set the stones into the fresh concrete surface before it hardens. You can work from prepared sketches or "wing it," laying them where you feel is right. Bury each pebble in concrete more than half way to be sure it won't work out. Freezing weather is tough on pebble mosaics, so be prepared for some pop-outs. Saved, these can easily be reset with epoxy glue.

Pebble paving is a Japanese art. But, unless you set them in mortar, you'll have a continual job replacing strays. Even then, some stones may work loose and have to be re-cemented with epoxy glue. Large pebbles such as these are suitable for walking on but not as a floor for outdoor furniture.

Exposed-aggregate concrete can be combined with pebble paving, which is simply another form of exposed aggregate. The large squares were done first, then the spaces filled.

A smoother pebble paving job is done by spreading mortar over a concrete slab, then inserting stones into it at random before the mortar sets up. A cracked concrete patio should be reclaimed in this fashion.

Here slabs of cut stone, scraps actually, were laid on a subbase and exposed-ag concrete placed around them. Similarly, old broken sidewalk pieces, log rounds, or railroad ties could have been incorporated into the concrete slab.

Redwood end blocks laid like bricks form a large pool deck/patio that will last a lifetime. The wood must be heartwood, however, for its extreme rot-resistance. Blocks are set carefully on a sand bedding with sand swept into the joints.

Liquid flooring. The outdoor equivalent of seamless flooring is now available for your deck or patio. Liquid-flooring resin and granules are squeezed and sprinkled on to form a tough and durable nonslip coating over the surface. Everything you need comes in proportioned cans. Select the colors to suit. Work in sections of about 50 sq. ft. at a time, applying a base coat first. At 70° F., this dries in about half an hour. Then spread the color mixture with a squeegee or trowel. When it levels out, sprinkle on additional granules of color. After a three- to six-hour cure, sweep off the loose granules and put on a clear coat of resin. Any time the surface shows wear, you can apply another coat of resin to brighten it up. For where-to-buy information, write Dur-A-Flex, Inc., 100 Meadow St., Hartford, Conn. 06114.

Elastobrick, stone. Other proprietary products called Elastobrick and Elastostone make a fine-looking and tough-wearing patio/deck flooring. They're made from a vinyl compound formed to look like brick or stone but acting and feeling like rubber. Each 2 by 2-foot sheet is ¼ to ½ inch thick and weighs 4½ pounds. Yet moisture absorption is almost nil. The soft, resilient feeling makes it ideal for use around swimming pools. Cost is moderate.

The tiles come in basket-weave brick pattern or flagstone (in 3 by 3-foot size). They can be laid over any solid surface and glued in place. Like other outdoor tiles, Elastobrick and stone can be hosed down for cleaning. Write to Structural Concepts, Inc., 5446 Satsuma Ave., North Hollywood, Calif. 91601, for details.

Sears deck. Not a patio-surfacing material, but a whole deck in kit form, is a new product sold by Sears & Roebuck. It consists of a 4 by 8-foot steel deck frame that you can assemble with wrench and electric drill. The deck stands on four steel legs. Each leg can be adjusted individually for height so the frame may be leveled on sloping or uneven ground. Sheet steel keeps the deck from rocking and swaying. Assembly instructions and hardware come with the kit, which sells for about $50. Ask for No. 64 KY 52417N. Decking lumber, railing, and stair kit are extra.

Rotproof deck. A precast concrete block deck was created and built by Miracle Adhesives Corp.'s board chairman Lloyd R. Cutler. Cutler used company adhesives to hold the lightweight precast concrete deck panels to their block foundation. He

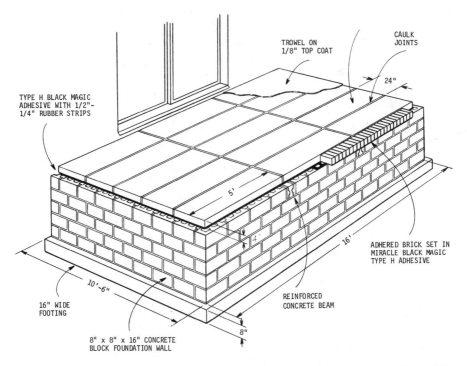

ROTPROOF, FIREPROOF CONCRETE DECK

offers to share the unusual design with readers. If you want a maintenance-free, fireproof add-on deck for your house, here it is.

The precast concrete beams and lightweight concrete deck slabs can be made at home but are better purchased from a concrete-products precaster (see your Yellow Pages). If you make the beams, use ordinary concrete in plywood forms. They should be four inches thick — they can be thinner throughout the center to save weight — 12 inches deep, and 10 feet long. Use plenty of reinforcing bars, equal to five percent of the weight of concrete. Deck slabs should be made of lightweight reinforced concrete 4 inches thick, 2 feet wide and 5 feet long. Lightweight concrete is made by using expanded aggregates such as perlite, haydite, cinders, or slag in place of sand and gravel.

If there is any question whether your beams and slabs can support the live weight of a 40-pound-per-sq.-ft. deck, better buy them professionally made. The concrete precaster should have tables indicating safe spans.

Cutler's assembled deck was given ⅛-inch-thick troweled-on mortar topping made by using Miracle cement additive MA 900 in place of the mix water in the mortar.

The entire assembly, with two men working, took just one hour, and Cutler says the porch is as good today as the day it was built — more than twenty-three years ago.

COMMON ALTERNATIVE MATERIALS FOR PAVING

TYPE	ADVANTAGES	DRAWBACKS	COST
Asphalt	Smooth, easily repaired	Softens in sun, hard to avoid "birdbaths", may be tracked in, needs edging	Low
Stones, chips, sawdust	Very easy to lay, easily redone, releveled	Collects dirt debris, may be tracked in, not for trafficked areas, needs confinement	Low
Adobe blocks	Lay like bricks, natural appearance	Needs uniform bedding, not for high-rainfall or frost areas	Moderate
Tile, rigid	Gives slick, formal appearance, permanent, high quality	High labor costs to lay, requires concrete, wood base	High
Tile, vinyl	Can carry indoors outside, easy to clean, easy to lay, colorful	Requires special adhesive, concrete, or wood base	Moderate
Carpeting	Can carry indoors outside, easy to lay, colorful, soft	Requires special carpet and adhesive, concrete, or wood base	Moderate
Log rounds, railroad ties	Rugged pattern often used with concrete between	Materials may be hard to find	Moderate

10 | Accessories

ACCESSORIES CAN MAGICALLY TRANSFORM your "Oh, it's just my backyard" into "Hey, let's go sit on my patio!" If it's the water that makes the beer, then certainly it's the accessories that make the patio or deck.

Choosing the right accessories for your patio/deck can be a problem, though. With advertisements and friends extolling the virtues of this or that, you wonder what is right for you. But a little thought and planning before you shell out for any accessory should pay off in the end.

If your patio or deck is still in the planning stages, first decide what you would like in the way of accessories and then what you can afford. If you already have one and want to add a few things, decide what's missing or lacking. Work from there. If the gap between what you want and what you can afford is considerable, think again. Maybe this or that accessory isn't quite right for you, or possibly you wouldn't get enough good out of it to justify the cost. Well-chosen accessories can return far more pleasure than their original cost.

You'll find the patio-accessories market crowded. A trip to a local garden or home center will prove that. Practically anything imaginable to improve the beauty and comfort of your deck or patio is available. A non-buying trip to one of these stores, pencil and paper in hand, may be worthwhile as a starter. Make a note of what you see that you might like to have. Don't be too critical at this point. Then when you get home, talk it over with the rest of the family and decide what everyone *really* wants and needs. Then return to buy, secure in the knowledge that the cash you're plopping down is for accessories you've thought out and are sure of.

Seating is an important part of every patio/deck, since most is designed with relaxation in mind. Among the most basic types of outdoor seating are the ever-present folding chairs and lounges. Most are made of lightweight materials such as aluminum, and can just as easily be thrown in the back of the car for a trip to the beach or a vacation in the mountains. They are reasonably comfortable, inexpensive, and are a good start for a budding outdoor living area.

More permanent are the built-in benches, which can be of stone, brick, or wood. An extra-wide wall of a low planter would make a good bench.

Backyard cookouts on warm summer evenings are fun; these are made possible using a portable hibachi, a stationary pit, or above-ground barbecue. Then if your activities attract any pesky mosquitoes, an electric bug-exterminator takes the sting out of them.

A set of free-standing patio torches creates an atmosphere of warmth on a cool evening (see Chapter 11).

You can leave a space in a patio, dig out a little bit, throw in some sand, and you've built a kid's sandbox.

American Plywood Assn.

Storage space for gardening tools or what-not abounds under the hinged panels of this carpeted patio deck. Hollow benches could also be adapted for hidden storage, or wall cabinets built to clear a patio/deck of clutter.

3M Co.

This device, a ground-fault circuit interrupter, detects ground-circuit leakage in an electrical appliance. If the currents differ by a hazardous level, the circuit is broken instantly, protecting against possible electrical shock. All new outlets must have this protection.

If you're not the green-thumb type, all kinds of artificial shrubbery and plants are available. And if you *are* a green thumber, there's nothing like planters to set off the beauty of your work.

To complete your deck/patio, how about adding a sundial? Or an old-fashioned swing? Or a screened veranda that gives relief from midday sun and flies, making a great place to retreat with a book or just your thoughts.

Few accessories enhance the appeal of a patio or deck more than its own built-in barbecue. The options are numerous. Choose from above-ground, like this brick one, or a barbecue pit. Some homeowners even pipe theirs for natural-gas operation, but today, charcoal or wood is more practical.

Planters such as this can be built any size you wish to help fill an empty corner. The splash of color from flowers or other foliage works wonders in a drab area. Planter decorations use up wood scraps.

Western Wood Products Assn.

National Concrete Masonry Assn.

Built-in benches should be suited to the peculiarities of your patio or deck. This design could easily be adapted to any plan. It is simply a supporting framework of 2 × 12s topped by a cap of 2 × 3s.

If you enjoy creative projects, why not try an interesting one like this, made of 2 × 6s and concrete blocks? Possibilities for a free-form design are endless. It could be a planter, a display pedestal or just a fill-in for an odd-shaped space.

Your patio or deck can be as elaborate as you like. Sauna bath, wading pool, or splashing fountain all thrill the senses. Or how about adding a wishing well?

In short, your outdoors can be whatever you want—and your pocketbook can pay for. Often, the addition of outdoor-living accessories, inexpensive or not, simple or elaborate, is the difference between a backyard and a genuine deck or patio.

Selective, electronic bug killer makes outdoor living more fun. Ultraviolet light attracts bugs. Inner energized grid is protected by an outer screen. Flies, mosquitoes, and moths fly through the screen and are killed while children, pets, and butterflies are unaffected.

You can have shade and sunshine, too, with a retractable residential awning. What's more, solar-heat input to the house is not affected while the awning isn't being used. Do-it-yourself installation is easy, since the rails simply screw to the house walls.

Flowtron/Automatic Radio

Carefree of Colorado

11 | Outdoor Lighting

WELL-PLANNED OUTDOOR LIGHTING extends the use of your patio or deck while providing additional general illumination for safety. A well lighted house and surrounding area discourages burglars.

Outdoor night lighting is not intended to provide a flat, even lighting as the sun would, but more to illuminate certain areas in a pleasing manner. Gentle, well-placed lights can accomplish this without any harshness. Further lighting serves only to enhance interesting garden and shrubbery areas or a pool.

Heating a patio or deck used to be desirable, also. Not any more. The cost of scarce fuel and power is going sky high; heating the outdoors is out.

TYPES OF OUTDOOR LIGHTING. There are several different systems of outdoor lighting: natural gas, and 120- and 12-volt electric systems. Each has its advantages and drawbacks. Not everyone has hookups for gas, at least not near the patio/deck. However, 120-volt current is most readily available to most outdoor living areas. A 12-volt system starts out with 120-volt power, steps it down for shock-safe, fire-safe outdoor use.

Lanterns, patio lamps, and torches using natural gas offer a warm feeling that's unobtainable with electric lighting. If you already have gas piped to an outdoor barbecue, half the work is done; you need only install additional fixtures and pipes. If not, you'll have to install gas lines to the general area first.

Electricity is available to most parts of your home, so it should not be hard to wire the patio or deck area. You can have switches inside the house for additional security as well as convenience. This way you can switch on your outdoor lights from inside without even being seen.

For even more versatility, you can install a 12-volt lighting system that plugs right into the 120-volt system. It offers increased safety, since you are dealing primarily with low-voltage wires and sockets. Also advantageous is economy in bulb replacement, and the ease of adding new fixtures. Wires are small and they may be exposed. The main component of the system is a transformer that converts 120 volts to 12 volts. A number of leads go from this main center to sockets: These are the low-voltage lights.

An exposed top-of-the-ground 12-volt installation is easily installed, and it permits you to put lights where you want them—on the ground, in trees, on the side of the house. If installed permanently, the 12-volt system takes the same amount of work as a 120-volt one. It's probably less expensive because of the lighter wires.

WHERE TO ILLUMINATE. You can put your outdoor lights just about anywhere you want them. Some locations are better than others. Travel paths and steps, especially, need illumination at night for convenience as well as safety. Low wide-

General Electric Co.

Lighting doubles the use of a patio or deck.
Pink lamps in the bubble and glow to faces.
Luminous panel (left) is a windbreak that lends
intrigue when sprinkled with colored lights
from behind. Both downlighting and uplighting
is used on garden and trees.

General Electric Co.

Nighttime conversational group is
created by two down floodlights in
the tree. The tree itself is lighted
from below with three floods. The
5' mushroom light illuminates a
planter box.

Large groups can be entertained informally on a lighted patio. The
area next to the house is lighted by
75-watt reflector lamps in deep
baffled units that are recessed in
the overhang. Three more units with
spread lenses are mounted together
in the tree to cast an interesting
shadow pattern on the patio.

General Electric Co.

Low-voltage lamps light a small
garden and patio area quite well.
Here they're used in both flood and
spot types, most concealed, although this isn't always necessary
or desirable. Recessed in the roof
overhang are 25-watt 12-volt
PAR36 floodlamps.

pattern lamps next to a walkway give the best illumination. The nicest units are housed in mushroom-type shells that direct light downward, showing all surface irregularities yet keeping light out of people's eyes. These also blend in with shrubbery and can be almost hidden within plantings. Recessed lighting mounted in the sides of the wall surrounding steps or walks become helpful permanent fixtures.

Illuminating surroundings. If your patio or deck is surrounded by gardens, you may want to show these off with some strategic lighting. A tree with interesting branch structure lends a nice effect when lighted from below with a small concealed spotlight.

Low, horizontal lights on the garden edge will show off planting areas. Spotlights cast shadows and illuminate pretty flowers in the garden. If placed away from the main area, these lights lend a more three-dimensional effect to the entire patio/deck area.

Around the barbecue. The barbecue, as the focal point of many patios and decks, is a prime target for lighting. Wide floodlight illumination in the area combined with a spotlight on the grill will make outdoor eating more enjoyable anytime. Small fringe lights will define the area slightly, and lend space at dinnertime.

If the barbecue is near the house, under-eave lighting provides general illumination. In food-preparation areas, a yellow "no-bug" lamp should be used to keep bothersome insects from gathering around it. A white floodlight can be used farther out to lead them away from the dining place.

Oriental-style hanging lamps give soft light and lend subdued informality. They can be strung from tree to tree around the barbecue area or wherever else that soft light is wanted.

Around the house. If your house is well built, there's no reason not to show it off at night, also. Floodlights placed to display some characteristic of the house will provide general illumination. A floodlight near a wall can show texture by creating interesting shadow patterns. Under-eaves lighting gives a sharp eave line, provides illumination for the surrounding area and shows off some of your home's structure. These are also useful from inside the house to illuminate anyone who approaches at night.

The easiest way to determine your needs for patio/deck lighting is to try moving a few small light sources on extension cords to the different areas where you think you might want lights. This will show, without making a permanent installation, the best placements for final fixtures. Then you can choose the fixtures suited to your needs, and figure out the materials needed.

FIXTURES. Many different types of outdoor lamp fixtures are available to accomplish different tasks in lighting your patio/deck. Basic lampstands for spotlights are usually hidden in trees or under the eaves for indirect lighting. Some are available with adjustable swivel necks for aiming the light. Still others have louvers aimed downward to provide light on the ground, not disturbingly up into the eyes.

Many small lamps are disguised as leaves, flowers, or other natural-appearing shapes to blend with a garden or foliage. Most of these have spikes that anchor them firmly in the ground for a temporary installation. These can also be installed in a conduit for permanent use.

Almost any type of exterior can be matched to your patio/deck lighting needs. Some lights look like bird houses and hang from tree limbs, casting a circle of light. Others sit on the ground and appear as stumps while they uplight a tree or shrub.

There are unlimited possibilities in using your own ideas to create lamp housings. Flowerpots, jars, or sprinkling cans may be altered to hold and direct a light source in an interesting manner. If you do this, either use a safe 12-volt system or build your housing around 120-volt fixtures that are weather-tight for outside use. Never try to make an outdoor fixture out of one designed for indoor use. That could cause a fatal shock. If there is any doubt, consult an electrician or your power company.

For long life and good service, outdoor fixtures should be made of heavy-duty materials and soundly constructed. Durability and weather-resistance are prime considerations in choosing outdoor lamps.

Steel, brass, copper, bronze, aluminum, and hard plastic fixtures are most suitable for this use. Most are painted dark green or black with white undersides to reflect light. These will blend easily with most settings, and especially well in gardens and shrubbery.

When selecting fixtures, be sure to look for ease in cleaning and changing bulbs. You may have to do this more often than you think.

Floodlights and spotlights usually have adjustable holders and weather-resistant projector (PAR) bulbs. Some have adjustable hoods that can direct light anywhere it is desired. Light bulbs for fixtures range from high-intensity spotlights and area lamps to low-illumination small-area lights. They come in many different colors, useful in illuminating foliage. Incandescent bulbs of the common household type come in all different sorts of holder shapes and colors. They can best be selected by determining how they fit in with your gardening or patio/deck scheme.

DETAILS OF UNDERGROUND OUTDOOR WIRING

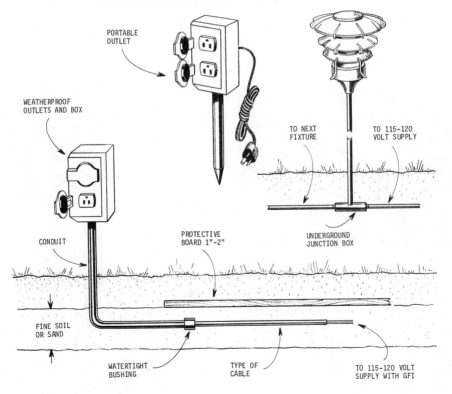

PORTABLE OUTLET

WEATHERPROOF OUTLETS AND BOX

TO NEXT FIXTURE

TO 115-120 VOLT SUPPLY

CONDUIT

PROTECTIVE BOARD 1"-2"

UNDERGROUND JUNCTION BOX

FINE SOIL OR SAND

WATERTIGHT BUSHING

TYPE OF CABLE

TO 115-120 VOLT SUPPLY WITH GFI

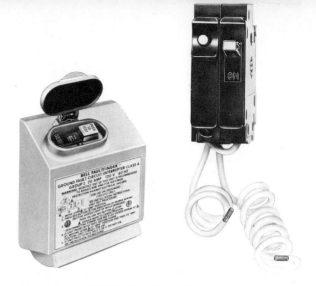

A must for outdoor-wiring circuits is a ground-fault interrupter (GFI). This one, by Hubbell, mounts on the outside wall of the house protecting electrical equipment plugged into it.

Another type of GFI is the Bell Faultfinder, which mounts outdoors on an outlet box. Plugs go in protected receptacles at the bottom. I-T-E Instant-Shield GFI circuit breaker fits into two standard breaker openings in a service panel. The entire circuit is thus protected.

Two General Electric 150-watt PAR (with self-reflector) lamps are mounted high on the side of the house to illuminate rock steps. These open-type lamps should mount higher than 10 feet if possible. Otherwise, louvered, deep-shielded fixtures should be used.

A tree with an open branch structure can be lighted from within as an after-dark focal point. Wide spread of the branches calls for use of an ordinary 100-watt household bulb in a weatherproof fixture instead of a PAR lamp. Diffusing plastic is being added for increased light spread.

General Electric Co.

Nighttime view of garden area. Two 150-watt PAR floods on the house are aimed toward the garden for general lighting. Eagle's accent lighting hides in an oversized flowerpot. Pair of 150-watt PAR's are recessed in the sunken garden, while another delineates the pool's shape. Tiny 10-watt lamps border the pathway.

On-the-ground outdoor lighting fixture by Stonco Lighting is self-supporting on its concrete base. Wiring is fed up from below, using Type UF cable buried in the ground.

Exterior plug-in fixture by Stonco has a spike that can be driven into the ground. Fixture may also be mounted on an electrical-outlet box and its wire fed through the mounting plate. The socket takes a PAR floodlamp.

Four fixtures for 12-volt outdoor lights are shown, two standing types and two hanging types.

Stonco Lighting

INSTALLATION. Unless you know your way around electrical wiring, call an electrician to install a 120-volt system for you. Outdoor wiring not only exposes people to shock, it exposes them to dampness and good (bad) grounding. Errors in wiring can cause electrocution.

In any case, outdoor circuits should be wired through what's called a ground-fault-circuit interrupter (GFI). A GFI costs about $60, and takes the place of an ordinary circuit breaker. It shuts off the power should there be a danger of shock in the system. A test button lets you periodically check the GFI's operation.

If you do the job yourself, plan exactly where the GFI, and any switches and outlets go. Measure the amount of electric cable and conduit (for above-ground parts) you will need. Use the type of wiring required by local code. And make your installation conform to the National Electric Code, latest edition. You can probably get a copy at your local library.

If you use easy nonmetallic cable, be sure to use *Type UF* (for direct burial in the ground). The cheaper *Type NM* is for indoors only.

Lay out the whole project on the ground as it will be located, to make sure you have all the necessary items. Bury the wires, install conduits where the wires leave the ground, and boxes for fixture connections. Pour concrete around the conduits to make them secure.

You may as well add convenience receptacles while you're at it. Since they're not switched, separate circuits might be needed. The wires can share their trenches, though.

Only after everything is connected properly and checked should you turn on the power. It's best to get a qualified electrician to check your work before you close things up.

Instructions for handling low-voltage outdoor-lighting systems are usually packed with the kit. You can get kits with six, 12, or more lamps. Follow the instructions for locating the master power unit, as well as connecting other components.

Go to it—having a lighted outdoor living area adds hours to the pleasure you'll get from it, plus value to your house.

12 | Building Stairs

LEVEL CHANGES CANNOT BE AVOIDED in many patios and decks. Unless these are smaller than about eight inches, you'll need stairs. These can take many forms. A gently sloping level change can be accommodated by terracing your entire patio or deck to follow the level. Each section or terrace is built close to the ground, one below the next, with the level changes held to about seven inches maximum.

Instead of building the whole thing terraced, you can make sloping steps leading from one level to another. Other times, there's a downright big difference in elevation; then you need honest-to-goodness stairs. If only one step is needed, this is often made by building an inverted box. Its level should be exactly halfway between the lower and upper levels.

In no case should the level change from one step to another by more than seven inches. This is called the *rise* of the step. The horizontal distance of the step is called its *run*. The minimum run of an outdoor step should be 11 inches. The rise and run must also be in proportion to each other for safe, comfortable use. Here's a rule of thumb: Two times the rise plus the run in inches should equal 23 to 25 (58-64 in centimeters). Another stairs rule: rise times run in inches should equal 70 to 75; in centimeters, 452 to 484.

Take an ideal $6\frac{1}{2}$-inch rise (15.2 cm) and 11-inch run (28 cm). It figures $2 \times 6\frac{1}{2} = 13 + 11 = 24$ — acceptable. Or $6\frac{1}{2} \times 11 = 71\frac{1}{2}$, also acceptable under the other rule.

The rise and run of each step in a stairway must be the same all the way up. Otherwise the user is apt to trip. Building inspectors often measure these and refuse to approve a set of stairs if there's more than a $\frac{1}{8}$-inch variation in any step. That isn't much tolerance, but you can achieve it.

One more stair rule has to do with steepness. Steep stairs are sometimes necessary, but they're not as safe as gently sloping stairs. Never should the rise be greater than the run, however. Any steep stairs need railings for safety.

To calculate the rise and run of each step in your stairway, you first need to know the total rise and total run to have to work with. Remember, to avoid steepness, use enough run to reach that $6\frac{1}{2}$:11 ideal rise:run, if you can. If not, use all of the run you can.

Now divide the total rise by $6\frac{1}{2}$. Rounded off, that's the ideal number of rises to have. Divide the number of steps into the total rise and finally you have the required rise of each step. Make them all the same.

Usually, a set of stairs uses the upper level for its top tread. Therefore, it contains one more rise than run. So divide the total stair run by the number of rises minus one. That gives the depth of each tread. Check your calculated rise and run through the rules of thumb. If they check out and you're satisfied with them, that part of your stairway is designed.

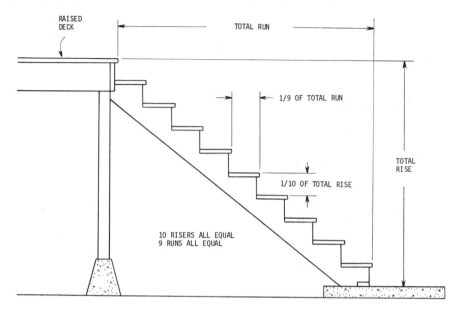

RISED
DECK

TOTAL RUN

1/9 OF TOTAL RUN

1/10 OF TOTAL RISE

TOTAL
RISE

10 RISERS ALL EQUAL
9 RUNS ALL EQUAL

RISE AND RUN OF STAIRS

Suppose, for example, that the total rise you have to work with is 4 feet 8 inches (56 inches) (142.2cm) and the total run is 5 feet 11¾ inches (71¾ inches) (181cm). Dividing the total rise by 6½ gives 8.6+ steps. You decide to go with 8 steps making each rise exactly 7 inches (17.8cm). That makes for 7 treads. So, 71¾ inches of total run divided by the 7 treads makes each tread come out 10¼ inches (26cm). The combination checks out using both rules of thumb.

Minimum stair width outdoors should be 39 inches (1m). Handrails, if used, should be about 31 inches (78.7cm) vertically from the tread leading edges.

WOOD STAIRS. These rules apply to both wood and concrete stairs. With wood stairs, which are the easiest to build, you have a choice of methods. In each, the treads are supported by members called stringers. Stairs more than 3 feet 6 inches wide (1.07m) and commonly using 2 × 10 or 2 × 12 lumber for treads need at least one more stringer up the middle of the stairway.

Cleats method. At the ends, the treads may be held by cleats—pieces of 2 × 2 wood blocking nailed to the stringers (see drawing). The stringer not only supports the stairs, it serves as an edging for them. Stringers like this are usually 2 × 8, better yet 2 × 10 lumber. Lines for cleat positioning are drawn onto each stringer using a carpenter's framing square as shown in the drawing. Tread nosings are usually set flush with the edge of the stringer when they are nailed to their cleats. A center support, if used, must be made using one of the other two methods.

Blocking method. Here, triangular wood blocks are cut from a 2 × 6 plank and nailed onto the stringers to hold the treads. The drawing shows how the cutouts are measured using a framing square and the known rise and run of each step.

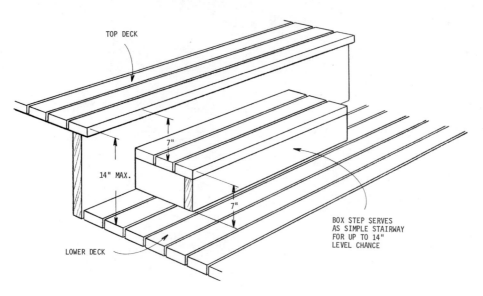

TOP DECK

7"

14" MAX.

7"

BOX STEP SERVES
AS SIMPLE STAIRWAY
FOR UP TO 14"
LEVEL CHANCE

LOWER DECK

BOX STEP

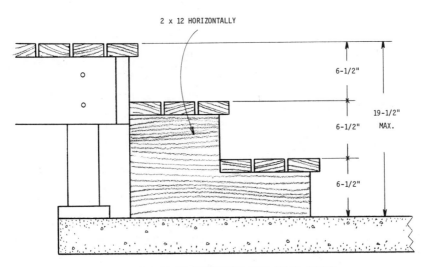

2 x 12 HORIZONTALLY

6-1/2"

19-1/2"
MAX.

6-1/2"

6-1/2"

2 × 12 ON EDGE NOTCHED FOR TWO STEPS

135

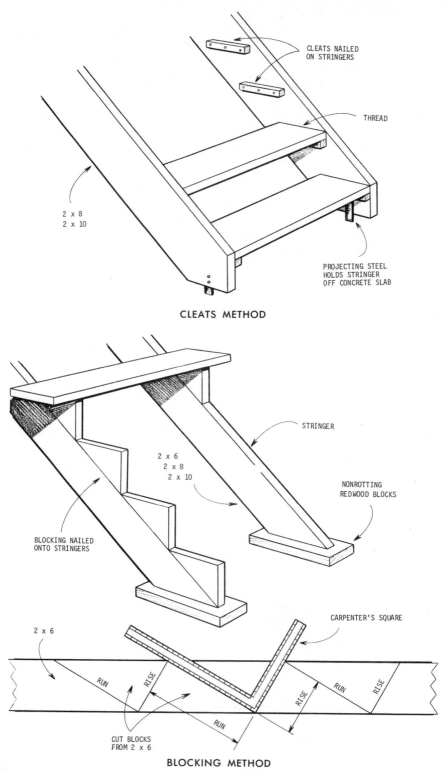

CLEATS NAILED
ON STRINGERS

THREAD

2 x 8
2 x 10

PROJECTING STEEL
HOLDS STRINGER
OFF CONCRETE SLAB

CLEATS METHOD

STRINGER

2 x 6
2 x 8
2 x 10

NONROTTING
REDWOOD BLOCKS

BLOCKING NAILED
ONTO STRINGERS

CARPENTER'S SQUARE

2 x 6

RUN

RISE

RISE

RUN

RISE

RUN

CUT BLOCKS
FROM 2 x 6

BLOCKING METHOD

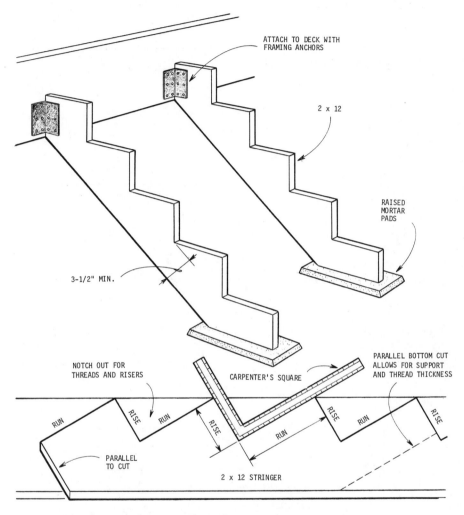

ATTACH TO DECK WITH
FRAMING ANCHORS

2 x 12

RAISED
MORTAR
PADS

3-1/2" MIN.

NOTCH OUT FOR
THREADS AND RISERS

CARPENTER'S SQUARE

PARALLEL BOTTOM CUT
ALLOWS FOR SUPPORT
AND THREAD THICKNESS

RUN   RISE   RUN   RISE   RUN   RISE   RUN   RISE

PARALLEL
TO CUT

2 x 12 STRINGER

NOTCHING METHOD

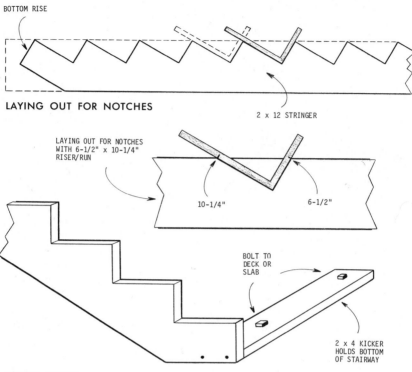

LAYING OUT FOR NOTCHES

2 x 12 STRINGER

LAYING OUT FOR NOTCHES
WITH 6-1/2" x 10-1/4"
RISER/RUN

10-1/4"

6-1/2"

BOLT TO
DECK OR
SLAB

2 x 4 KICKER
HOLDS BOTTOM
OF STAIRWAY

KICKER DETAIL

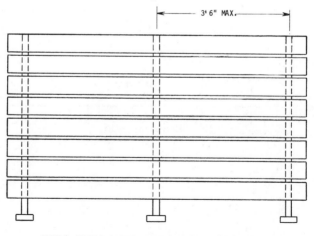

3' 6" MAX.

WIDE STEPS NEED ADDITIONAL STRINGERS

138

Notching method. The most commonly used method especially for shorter stair-ways where the resultant weakening of the stringer doesn't matter. A framing square is used to mark off notching cuts for rise and run all the way up the stringer. The first mark is a horizontal cut at the bottom, and the last is a vertical cut at the top to fit the riser to the stairway. Both cuts are marked using the framing square. The horizontal cut is naturally parallel to the treads; the vertical cut is, of course, parallel to the risers. All stringers are cut the same, and are set in slightly from the ends of treads.

Notched stringers must start out wide enough to have at least $3\frac{1}{2}$ inches (8.9cm) of effective width below the notches. This usually calls for the use of 2×12 lumber.

In each method, treads wider than called for by your runs may be used by letting the top of the one tread overlap the bottom of the other. The rise and run are unaffected. Marking and notching are no different, except that the top vertical cut must allow for this.

Stringers are usually attached to the deck at the top with simple framing anchors. At the bottom, they rest on nonrotting wood supports on the ground or on raised mortar pads on a concrete slab. They may also be supported about an inch off the ground by bolting them to heavy steel bars projecting out of a concrete slab. Of course, the stringers must be cut properly at the bottom to allow for the method of support used. In any case, don't let stringers rest on concrete or on the ground. They'll soon rot or attract termites.

Some system for anchoring the stairs at their bottom is needed so they don't slide from side to side. You can stake them to the ground or bolt a nonrotting 2×4 kicker to a concrete slab at that location. The steel-projection method both supports and anchors at the same time.

Treads are often made of 2×12 boards cut to the desired length. Ganged-up 2×4s may also be used, but they don't make so trim a job. Often, no risers are used and the stairs are left open between treads.

CONCRETE STAIRS. Short level changes are not too hard to build in concrete. Form steps as shown in the drawing, leaving the tread areas exposed for trowel-finishing. Old bricks, concrete blocks and other solid rubble may be thrown inside the forms to save on concrete. Keep this fill at least two inches back from the surface of the steps. Make your pour all at one time, avoiding "cold" joints in the concrete.

The professional's step-finishing system is to take off the riser forms when the concrete gets stiff enough to support itself. They finish the treads and risers using angled stair-finishing tools on the outside and inside corners of steps. If you wait a lit-tle too long, however, the concrete will be too far set for good finishing. And if you strip the forms too soon, huge chunks of the steps will slough away. I recommend the amateur's method: wood-floating-finish the tops of the steps. As best you can, reach in under the bottom of each riser form with a trowel blade to finish it. Use an edger to round off the nosings, but leave the risers with a formed finish. Strip the forms only after a week's curing.

In any case, to get a smooth exterior finish, tap around the wood forms right after placing the concrete mix in them. This helps eliminate air bubbles.

The accompanying photos show other kinds of stairs you can make for your patio or deck. They're probably the simplest of all to do.

Handsome stairs are built of split concrete blocks and precast concrete tiles. Set tiles, lay up two rows of blocks, set more tiles, etc. The whole job is a day's work once the materials have been assembled.

Cement and Concrete Assn.

Entire patio, including the steps, was made of precast concrete units cast against a rough surface that made them look like stones. Units were set on sand using the mortarless method. Split concrete-block edgings laid in an ashlar pattern add to the formal appearance.

Cement and Concrete Assn.

Bricks set on concrete in 2 × 6 wood frames cantilever out from one another in an informal and attractive arrangement. These stairs are much easier for the weekend mason to build than the cast-in-place, trowel-finished ones. And they look every bit as good.

1. Forming for a concrete stairway doesn't look very pretty. It's what the end product looks like that counts. Bracing is required to take the pressures when fresh concrete is placed in the forms. Later all is removed.

BUILDING CONCRETE STAIRS

2. Concrete is placed and finished level with the tops of the riser forms. Edging tool gives the steps a rounded nose to prevent chipping. Treads shouldn't be troweled too smoothly to be slippery.

3. When the step concrete has set sufficiently, the riser forms are removed carefully so that the risers can be troweled smooth. We recommend that this step and the next one be skipped. The fresh steps are likely to crumble.

4. Professional cement finisher trowels the fronts of the risers with a sponge-rubber float. Sometimes a sand-cement mix is spread onto the risers before finishing them.

5. Stair corners are finished with a corner tool made especially for this job. It is very difficult for a beginning finisher to turn out a job that looks this well.

6. Completed concrete steps, when professionally built, are a credit to the house, need no maintenance.

13 | A Deck for Your Pool

IF YOU HAVE AN ABOVE-GROUND SWIMMING POOL, sooner or later you'll want some sort of deck to go with it. A deck gives such a pool the feel of an inground pool at little additional cost. It makes a place for people to gather, dry off, sun themselves between dips. If large enough, it can double as a full deck for eating and entertaining. Even a minimum-size pool deck can be used for sitting around the pool when you're not swimming.

A number of pool manufacturers offer add-on deck kits made to fit their own pools and other above-ground pools. Basically do-it-yourself kits, they come with all the necessary materials: precut pieces, bolts, screws and assembly instructions. Kits are made for the most common pool shapes, rectangular, round, and oval. Most are metal —steel or aluminum; a few are wood. One model comes with the fittings: you buy the lumber and assemble it.

Of course you can easily design your own wooden pool deck, resting it on nonrotting wood pads on the ground. For beam and plank spans, spacing, and so on, use the tables in Chapter 5. The addition of 2 × 4 angle-braces in both longitudinal and lateral directions underneath the deck will prevent sway when you walk. Kit decks come with the necessary bracing.

Two add-on kits are shown for a Coleco Contempora Oval pool, one for the end deck and one for the fencing. Gate and climb-up ladder are part of the all-aluminum packages.

Small redwood-deck kit (also from Coleco) is designed for the side of an oval pool. Upright posts rest on nonrotting redwood blocks.

Coleco

Tiny fenced deck gives slightly more utility to a pool than a mere ladder would. Gate can be locked, thus preventing small children from using the pool while unattended. Deck may be ordered with the pool kit or added later.

You can choose from full, half, or quarter-round decks in various widths. A full deck in a large width will give more than enough room for most needs.

All but the smallest pool decks should have a railing for safety. Some kits come with the railing; in others the railing must be ordered separately. Some rails include a locking gate or swing-up ladder to keep children out of the pool when you're not around. The rail should be sturdy enough for you to lean or fall on it without crashing through.

A pool deck must also include a ladder for getting onto it, and ideally, another set of steps leading to the pool. Most do. If not, you can order these separately. Many above-ground pools are not for diving, so you enter from the ladder.

Whether you order simply a wide pool edging or an all-round sundeck is a matter of cost and convenience. I feel that the most practical arrangement is to have an 8-foot sundeck at one end of the pool, plus an all-around 2-foot-wide fenced walkway. That way pool users can get out of the pool onto the walkway at any point. The large deck is available for drying and lounging.

Like an above-ground pool, a deck is not considered by the tax assessor to be a permanent improvement to your property, so it shouldn't increase your property valuation and add to your tax bill. On the other hand, it won't increase the market value of your house and grounds the way an inground pool with deck would. But should you sell your house, it might just make the difference between a prospect and a buyer. We don't recommend moving an above-ground pool and deck, even though that is technically possible. It's simply too much work for what you get. Better to buy a new pool and deck when you get where you're going.

If you are starting from scratch and erecting an above-ground pool, there's no need to order the pool and deck together. Get the pool up and working, then get the deck kit for it and build that on. Some pools, though, come with the deck as an integral part of the structure. In that case, you must assemble the two together, since the deck is supported by the pool walls and they, in turn, are braced by the deck.

Few tools are needed to assemble a deck kit other than a screwdriver and a pair of pliers or small open-end wrench. A push-pull screwdriver will save a lot of wrist action in running the many screws that most kits contain. With a little help, you should have the whole job done the same day.

14 | Edges for Patios and Decks

PATIO AND DECK EDGINGS serve many purposes. Aside from good design, a well-planned and constructed edging adds safety, privacy, and windbreak, and divides your space. A handsome edging becomes an asset to your property, adding appreciable value along with its usefulness.

Elevated patio/decks—those more than about 18 inches high—need something reasonably solid around the outside perimeter to keep people from falling off. A sturdy picket fence would do the job quite well, as would a brick or wood wall. Height should be about 42 inches (check your code).

Wrought-iron railings are particularly suitable. They allow visibility, but restrain children and others from falling. Iron railings are offered in many attractive styles.

For a windbreak fence, a wall or a planting helps considerably. If a calm patio/deck area is what you're after, a protective wall or fence on the windy side will soften the blasts. Slatted or louvered fences let gentle breezes flow through; solid walls create a relatively breeze-free area. Thick stands of small shrubs will also break the wind and lend a natural appearance to your patio/deck setting.

Patio/deck edgings can also serve to divide an outdoor area, and to separate different functions, if desired. Low walls of wood, rock, or brick keep leaves and debris from blowing in. These will appear compatible if you use the same materials and treatments as in your house.

Space dividers of rugged lumber offer a rustic quality, and are functional, too. Planter boxes can be built in them to add greenery to outdoor living.

Fences of all types are available for the choosing. Wood, aluminum, and combinations of these with translucent plastic panels make striking additions. Anodized-aluminum fences never need painting, last a lifetime, and come in a large selection of colors.

A good grade of fence wood will last a long time. Depending on the desired effect, wood walls or fences can be left unfinished, stained almost any color, or painted—affording a wide range of results. Staining lasts longest and requires the least maintenance. Avoid clear finishes: They hardly last at all.

A tall fence placed on a common property line will give you privacy. Possibly, your neighbors may help you with the cost and labor of installing one, as it will benefit them, too. This type of fence should be made with extra attention to design, since both families will have it as a permanent wall. It's best to have a written agreement covering ownership and maintenance.

With the many types of patio/deck edgings available, your ideas can be accomplished readily. If you're a plant lover, use lots of planters. Or work with rustic wood if that's the effect you want. Almost any combination is possible to suit your patio/deck needs. The photos on these pages give lots of ideas. Use them, if you wish.

Three kinds of edgings for a brick patio combine to give a feeling of enclosure. Wrought-iron railing is formal, brick barbecue utilitarian, and wood rail fence is informal.

Outdoor fence made by nailing western red cedar 1 × 2s up flat to make the pattern, then sliding the nailed-up section into slots in the cedar fence posts.

Courtyard was built in place of a straggly strip of lawn and fenced to shut out the view of an ugly street. Wall of stained resawn cedar has its boards recessed from the posts for shadow lines.

Low concrete-block fence is made formal by sectioning it into 8' lengths, adding screen-block dividers and topping it off with wrought iron. A cast-concrete foundation is needed.

Home-built fence using flat Filon panels in varied colors stops the wind and view but lets light and shadow patterns show through. The plastic material comes in rolls or sheets, cuts with an ordinary saw.

A screen-block wall is easily built by the home mason using a vertical post at each end and a stringline stretched between them for laying each course. The job goes best with ready-packaged mortar mix. All you add is water, then mix, spread and lay the grille blocks.

Sakrete

The finished job looks good enough to eat. Screen block walls let breezes through and give privacy as well as beauty. A concrete footing is needed.

A patio edging needn't be high to be effective. Low split-concrete block wall does a fine job of outlining, separating a patio area from a planting area. Lay it on a concrete footing.

Six-sided grille blocks (made in England) lay up to make a formal honeycomb-screen wall. Half blocks are used at the ends in every other course. Starter and cap blocks are also used.

Plywood fence stained dark oak and fitted with stained rough-cedar battens delineates space and adds privacy to a brick patio. It is supported by nonrotting posts 4 feet apart.

Upper-level deck and walkway are edged with rough-sawn plywood panels to keep children and animals from getting through and falling. Code requirements for railing height should be followed.

American Plywood Assn.

Wood Products Assn.

Mobile-home patio is edged with maintenance-free stained-cedar boards made to match the walkway. The landscaping treatment helps to make the mobile blend into its setting.

One of the lowest-cost and easily installed edgings is a woven picket fence. Special metal gates are available to go with it. It adapts to many purposes, offering utility and durability at reasonable cost.

Rowe Mfg. Co.

Gates through edgings are often needed. You can build them with style and grace. This one would be plain without the nailed-on wood trim over the edge-to-edge boards.

Western Wood Products Assn.

Rough sawn redwood 2 × 10s gang up to make a low edging for a patio. They're capped off by a longer 2 × 8. The bi-level feature could be carried on up a hill or used to build up from a low edging to a high fence.

California Redwood Assn.

15 | Roofing a Patio or Deck

Patios and decks need not be open to the air or full sunlight. A covered patio/deck can greatly extend the outdoor season. In the summer you can enjoy cooling breezes without being cooked by the sun. A winter cookout on a nice day can do wonders to relieve the shut-in feeling that goes with the season.

Two types of coverings are common: the open framework and the weathertight, fully covered roof. Each has advantages and drawbacks; both should be considered before a final choice is made.

OPEN-FRAMEWORK COVERINGS. These serve mainly to diffuse sunlight, allowing soft light and breezes through, while providing partial shade. You have the open-air feeling, but without excess sunlight.

A lathhouse roof is the most fundamental of open coverings. Constructed usually of 1 × 2s nailed over a sturdy framework, the laths cast interesting ribbed shadow patterns on the floor.

Egg-crate-grid covers are more open to the air than lathhouse types. They also cast interesting shadow patterns and provide some shade.

A trellis roof can be made from either a lathhouse or egg-crate patio/deck covering simply by growing and training vines over the framework. Plants such as Chinese wisteria, Easter-lily vine, and trumpet vine are effective in further shading your patio/deck, besides the natural beauty and fragrance they add.

Split or whole bamboo gives a natural lathhouse effect and is easy to put up. Palm-frond thatch roofs are also attractive, allow air circulation, and will even shed rainwater to some extent, if they're thick enough.

Open frameworks with adjustable panels allow you to regulate the quantity and location of sunlight you want on the patio or deck. Solid or lath-type panels slide on tracks in the open framework roof to give different areas of shade and light.

Louvers in the patio/deck roof let you control the amount of light, from almost complete shade to nearly full sunlight. Individual louvers are connected to a pole that adjusts with a single move. With this type, you can take full advantage of sky brightness and avoid direct sunlight by aiming the louvers away from the sun to give an open-shade effect.

FULLY WEATHERTIGHT COVERINGS. These act as an open-air extension of your house. Cross breezes flow through the shaded patio area, but rain need not discourage you from using your outdoors. Probably the simplest of this type of covering is merely an extension of your house's roof over the patio/deck area. Supported on posts, the roof covering may be the same as on your present roof to blend in. In construction, it is treated just as your house roof would be, down to the rain gutters and all.

Patio overhead made of 2 × 4s and lightweight bender boards makes interesting shadow patterns. The 2 × 4s attach to a 2 × 4 ledger strip on the house at one end and a 2 × 6 beam supported on posts away from the house. Bender boards create curving arches.

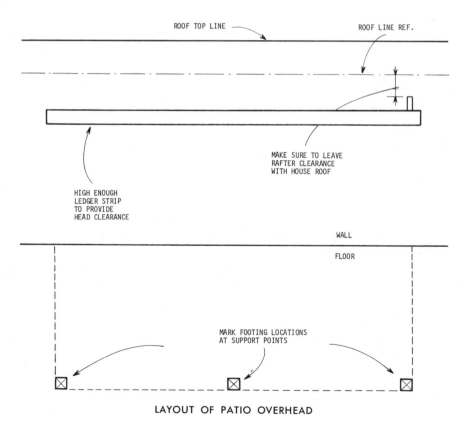

ROOF TOP LINE

ROOF LINE REF.

MAKE SURE TO LEAVE
RAFTER CLEARANCE
WITH HOUSE ROOF

HIGH ENOUGH
LEDGER STRIP
TO PROVIDE
HEAD CLEARANCE

WALL

FLOOR

MARK FOOTING LOCATIONS
AT SUPPORT POINTS

LAYOUT OF PATIO OVERHEAD

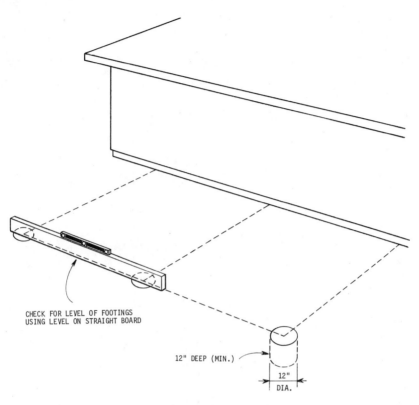

CHECK FOR LEVEL OF FOOTINGS
USING LEVEL ON STRAIGHT BOARD

12" DEEP (MIN.)

12"
DIA.

FOOTING PLACEMENT

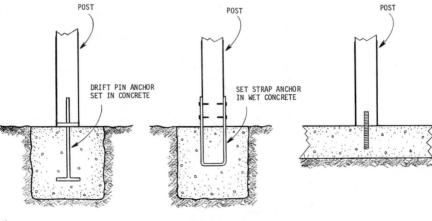

POST

POST

POST

DRIFT PIN ANCHOR
SET IN CONCRETE

SET STRAP ANCHOR
IN WET CONCRETE

ANCHOR METHODS

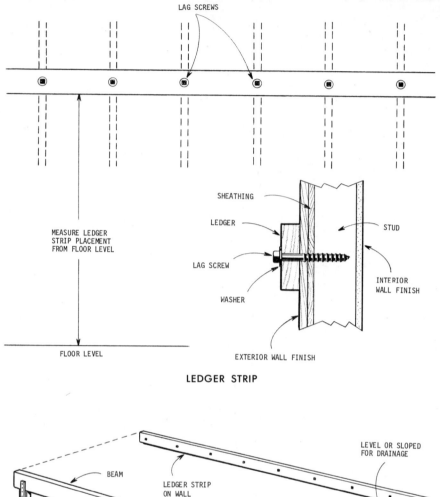

LAG SCREWS

MEASURE LEDGER
STRIP PLACEMENT
FROM FLOOR LEVEL

FLOOR LEVEL

SHEATHING

LEDGER

LAG SCREW

WASHER

STUD

INTERIOR
WALL FINISH

EXTERIOR WALL FINISH

LEDGER STRIP

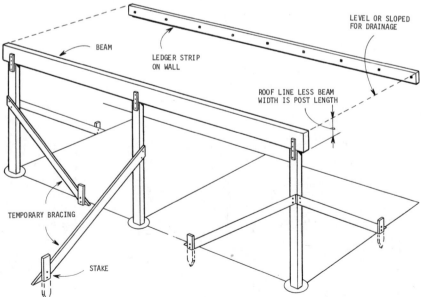

LEVEL OR SLOPED
FOR DRAINAGE

BEAM

LEDGER STRIP
ON WALL

ROOF LINE LESS BEAM
WIDTH IS POST LENGTH

TEMPORARY BRACING

STAKE

ERECTING THE POSTS

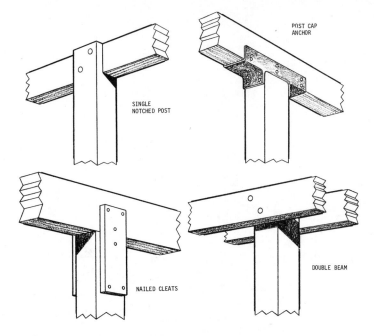

SINGLE
NOTCHED POST

POST CAP
ANCHOR

NAILED CLEATS

DOUBLE BEAM

POST AND BEAM CONNECTIONS

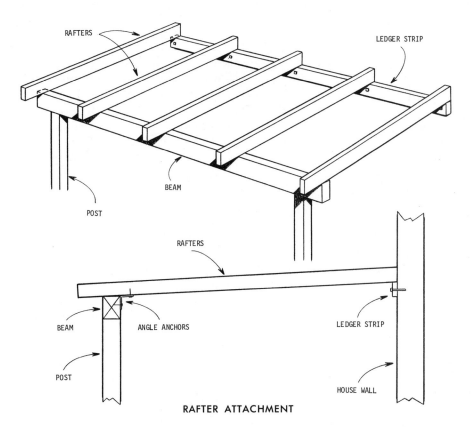

RAFTERS

LEDGER STRIP

POST

BEAM

RAFTERS

BEAM

ANGLE ANCHORS

LEDGER STRIP

POST

HOUSE WALL

RAFTER ATTACHMENT

REDWOOD PATIO COVERS

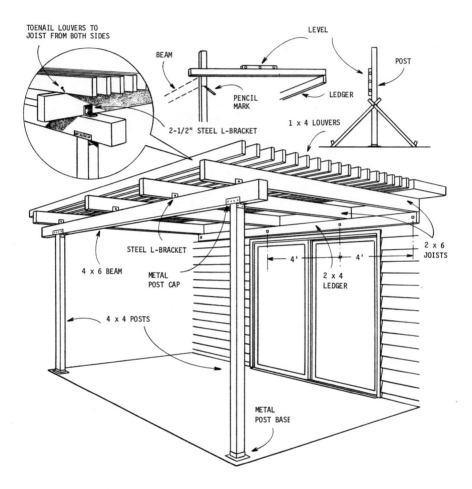

TOENAIL LOUVERS TO
JOIST FROM BOTH SIDES

BEAM

LEVEL

POST

PENCIL
MARK

LEDGER

2-1/2" STEEL L-BRACKET

1 x 4 LOUVERS

STEEL L-BRACKET

4 x 6 BEAM

METAL
POST CAP

4 x 4 POSTS

4'

4'

2 x 4
LEDGER

2 x 6
JOISTS

METAL
POST BASE

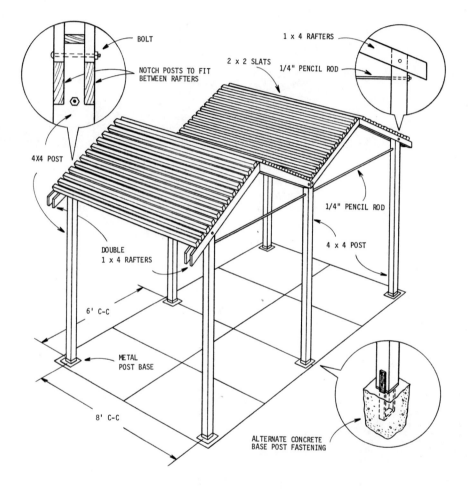

BOLT

NOTCH POSTS TO FIT
BETWEEN RAFTERS

1 x 4 RAFTERS

2 x 2 SLATS

1/4" PENCIL ROD

4X4 POST

1/4" PENCIL ROD

DOUBLE
1 x 4 RAFTERS

4 x 4 POST

6' C-C

METAL
POST BASE

8' C-C

ALTERNATE CONCRETE
BASE POST FASTENING

To make a lightweight translucent fiberglass patio cover, first erect the wood framework. The 2 × 6 joists spaced 24″ on centers are braced with 2 × 4 headers toenailed to them. Size of members depends on their span.

Then install the translucent striped panels. Note the wiggly moldings nailed across the framing to better support the corrugated panels. These may be purchased along with the panels. Do all panel nailing at the ridges, not in the gutters.

The finished job, using panels called Filon Stripes, is colorful. The panels can take sun, rain, and snow for years.

The finished Filon job lets light through for a pleasant under-cover effect. The stripes show through from the bottom to add color to your outdoor living.

Canvas awnings provide shade and are also weathertight. Cross breezes will circulate, but upward breezes will be impaired by the close weave of the fabric. One advantage of the canvas awning is its relative ease in setting up.

A new idea under the sun is using translucent roofing panels to cover all or part of your patio or deck. Made of sun-resistant fiberglass-reinforced plastic, these panels let in diffused light while providing a roof. A light, airy feeling is achieved by the soft light that penetrates. The vivid color combinations and pinstripes now available make these panels exciting to look at. The colors can be chosen to match the color schemes in your house, garden, or pool area.

Some of the many benefits of translucent roofing panels are low maintenance, weather resistance, shatter resistance and durability. A simple hosing-off cleans them because their smooth surface doesn't collect dirt easily.

Whether you will want an open, airy patio/deck covering or a fully weathertight roof depends mostly on personal preference and local weather. Figure out what times of the year you most like to use your patio/deck. If a covered patio/deck could extend these times, then it might be a worthwhile investment. If you use your patio normally all year long, weather permitting, then a fully weathertight patio covering would be most beneficial.

16 | Ferro-Furniture for Outdoor Living

YOU CAN BUILD real outdoor furniture yourself of ferro-cement. Ferro-cement is thin, strong, highly reinforced concrete using mesh reinforcement. A Ferro-cement structure is much stronger than either cement or mesh would be by itself. The material was discovered years ago by Italian architect Pier Luigi Nervi. He named it and used it to build undulating roofs on buildings without using forms,

You can build ferro-furniture simply by forming the mesh to the desired shape. Like the eggshell, ferro-furniture gets its strength not from thickness of its walls but from its curved shapes. No wood is used in ferro-cement, so there's nothing to rot. If you add coloring to the cement mix, you won't even have to paint the finished project. You can use ferro-cement to make the table shown. Or you can build a bench, chair, planter, birdbath, screen, garden fountain, or whatever else you'd like.

Whatever you build, sketch out the design first. Keep in mind that you're working in a new medium, and forget the limitations of wood and formed concrete. Use lots of curves. Don't use many flat planes because these lack natural strength. Keep all curves simple, avoiding surfaces with double curvatures, as these will be tough to form in mesh. Good are circles, cylinders, cones, scrolls, and free-form curving planes. How to build a sample project is shown in the photos.

Once the mesh shape is assembled and braced as necessary with ¼-inch reinforcing bars, try to guess where the greatest strain will occur. Put a light load on it and see where most of the bending comes. Wire on extra strips of metal lath at these points. Make the mesh three and four layers thick—thicker still if there's much bending. Pay particular attention to the joints between two planes. If the load of a seated person is to be transferred from one plane to another, a reinforcing strip of metal lath on the underside will help. In any case, it won't hurt, except to thicken the joint and add weight. Sheets of mesh may be fastened together or over-lapped to make larger surfaces.

The only real drawback to the whole process is handling that blasted metal lath. Its sharp edges cut your hands, skin your knuckles, snag clothing. Once you have the lath cut and shaped, the rest is simple.

Doubling the lath helps to make grout stay in place. You can save on cutting by folding the mesh, and walking on folds to flatten them. If mesh layers try to spring apart, a few well-placed tie-wires will tame them. Instead of the metal lath, you can use ¼-inch hardware cloth. But, as with the lath, you'll need at least a double layer to hold grout.

Anything goes during the cement-grouting operation. I found it easiest to grout with bare hands. Even though the alkali in cement will make your hands dry for several days afterward, it's worth it for easy grouting. If you can't stand cement on your hands, wear dipped gloves. Next best, I found, is to trowel the grout into the mesh with a flexible-blade plasterboard-jointing knife. Use one about six or eight inches wide. The knife is no use on curves; back to the hand method for them. Small mason's trowels work, but they are slow.

Two groutings are needed. The first one fills the mesh and creates a structure. The second, done a day or two later, protects the metal from corrosion and smooths the surface. If you follow the second coat while the first is still damp, no bonding agent is needed between the two. The second grouting layer need be no thicker than about $\frac{1}{8}$ inch.

You may mix your own grout using a 1:3 portland cement: fine sand mix. Or use a ready-packaged sand-mix (topping) product, such as Sakrete makes. Add just enough water to make the mix for grouting. Don't use mortar: It contains lime, which makes it plastic and workable but not strong enough for ferro-cement.

You can paint your project if it's not integrally colored. If people are to sit on it, be sure to use a nonchalking exterior type of paint that's compatible with concrete. Ask your paints dealer to recommend one.

The table shown in the photos is made with six sheets of plaster lath. The base is made with four sheets doubled, rolled into scrolls and tied to reinforcing rods bent to the desired shape. The table's top is formed of two sheets of metal lath folded and pieces together then filled out with scraps of mesh. A $1\frac{1}{2}$-inch rim made of folded-over mesh and wired on around the edge strengthens the top. No rebars are needed to make the top. The top and base are grouted separately, assembled loosely when finished.

Statistics on the table may help you in building it. The top weighs 74 pounds, the bottom 130 pounds. The bottom was overdesigned. Instead of sandwiching the rebars between layers of mesh, put them on the outside. Then the double lath layers will fit snugly together. This alone should lop off about 50 pounds, I estimate. The lighter base would still have plenty of strength. Panel cross-sections are about $\frac{3}{8}$ inch thick, about right.

In spite of being built of ferro-cement, the table is portable. To move it, lift off the top (a two-man job). One person can then roll it along on the rim, but the base must be carried.

When you've tried ferro-cement, you'll agree that working with this unusual material is totally different, mostly fun, and always challenging.

Maintenance-free planter-table is made by grouting double layers of metal lath with cement mix, then letting it harden to form ferro-cement. Color was mixed into the cement plaster.

Mark plasterer's metal lath for cutting, using a crayon or piece of chalk. Plan the job to make best use of the 28″ by 96½″ lath panels. Leather gloves protect hands from the prickly mesh.

Old chalk-on-a-string method of scribing a circle outlines the 47″-diameter mesh for the table top. Two panels of mesh have been wired together to make the wide top.

Best mesh cutting is done with aircraft snips that will cut right and left curves. Gloves are almost mandatory for this step. A little extra material is left for overlapping and tying with wire.

To save on cutting, bend panels over a piece of plywood into the desired sizes, then splice on pieces to fill them out. Cutting a 16″ by 47″ side panel, as you'll find, is the hardest part of the ferro-cement process.

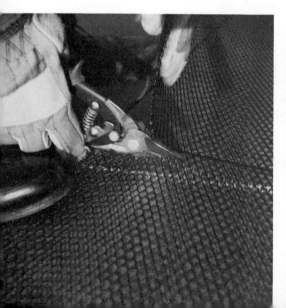

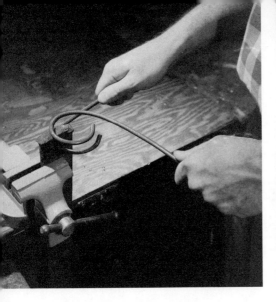

Form eight ¼" by 48" reinforcing rods to the scroll ends, making a single perfect one, then bending the others to match it. All are thus alike. Hole in a piece of steel clamped in the vise does a good job of bending.

Roll up both ends of each side-panel mesh around a 1½" pipe. This readies it for the scroll, which gives considerable strength to the finished structure. You'll have eight such single panels, doubled two per side.

Now tie-wire one section of metal-lath scroll to the top rebar. At this stage use only enough wires to hold it in place on the mesh.

Next install the other side panel, sandwiching it to the first. Design shows the rebar between the layers of mesh. (Better would be with the rebars outside of both layers.)

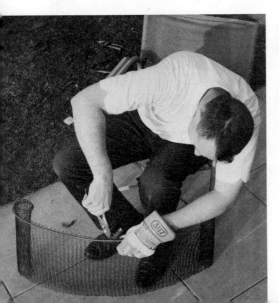

When all four side panels have been made up, erect the table's pedestal base by wiring all four panels together, using No. 16 mechanic's wire. Nip off twisted wire ends and tuck them out of the way inside the mesh layers.

Now you're ready to grout. Mix up a cement-sand mix using one part portland cement to three parts mortar sand. Add just enough water to make a workable mix. Midget mortar mixer takes the labor out of mixing.

The best way to work grout into the mesh is literally by hand. Keep going until all voids in the mesh have been filled with grout. Author did base in two stages, which allowed him to sit on the hardened portion.

With the mesh openings arranged facing downward, grout goes in easily by "troweling" up. Hand troweling works especially well on sharply curved portions. Wash the cement off your hands as soon as you finish.

Edges of ferro-cement panels need special attention to avoid corrosion of exposed mesh. Pack extra grout along the edges, rounding it off with your hands. Grout is hard on hands, so wash them and treat frequently with hand lotion.

Mark the interior cutout for the tabletop with your metal lath laid out on top of the curing base. Do it with chalk. Note the polyethylene sheeting wrapped around the base for curing.

Now cut out the interior opening with metal snips, following chalk lines made in the previous step. Here again, leather gloves will protect your hands from that murderous mesh. Two sheets of metal lath are wired together to make the top width.

Scraps of metal lath folded three layers thick over plywood form the 1½" rim around the tabletop. After folding, lay plywood on top of the folded strips and walk on it to flatten them.

Attach the triple-thick edging around the outside of the tabletop, wiring it every six inches or so. Make enough edging to go around the inside cutout, too, and attach it. Edging not only gives thicker appearance to the tabletop, it adds strength.

Lay mesh for top on a sheet of polyethylene and work grout into it. Working horizontally with the plastic as backing, this step goes quickly with a 6" flexible broadknife.

A good way to grout the tabletop edge is with a broadknife backed up with a wood float for concrete. As you grout, move both the broadknife and float around together. Make sure mesh isn't left exposed at the edges.

When the parts have hardened (they needn't be completely cured), the rough, exposed mesh can be covered by a second grouting. First brush on a coat of neat-cement paste (portland cement and water). Before this dries, apply grout.

You can have an attractive travertine texture on ferro-furniture by applying topping grout — it may be colored — then "smooshing" it up with your fingers, finally troweling over it lightly to smooth off the high spots.

Cure the top by covering it with a sheet of polyethylene plastic for about a week for a full cure. This step is important to achieve the full strength of the project.

The top weighs only 75 lb. (34 kg), but lifting it on and off the base is a two-man job. Base can be handled by one person. Lips of the inner cutout fit down inside the base, locking it on.

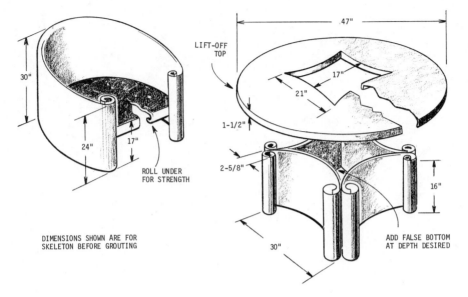

30"

24" 17"

ROLL UNDER
FOR STRENGTH

DIMENSIONS SHOWN ARE FOR
SKELETON BEFORE GROUTING

LIFT-OFF
TOP

47"

17"

21"

1-1/2"

2-5/8"

16"

30"

ADD FALSE BOTTOM
AT DEPTH DESIRED

FERRO-FURNITURE DIMENSIONS

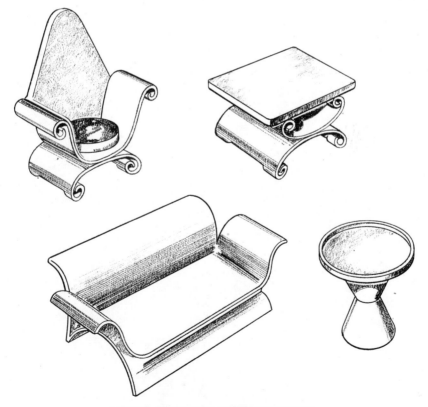

OTHER IDEAS FOR FERRO FURNITURE

Glossary of Outdoor Living

Arbor. Garden structure composed of a skeletal framework of pipe or light wood that supports an overgrowth of vines or climbing ivy. Provides an airy, open retreat in an isolated area of the yard. (*See* GAZEBO.)

Awning. A sun-sheltering device located over windows or doorways. Awnings are customarily made of canvas, reed, bamboo, or light lumber. Greater protection from the elements is afforded by aluminum, fiberglass, and other permanent materials.

Breezeway. A roofed passageway, often with open sides, designed to connect two structures (i.e., house and garage). Often it is screened to create a summertime dining area, play area for youngsters, or dog exercise area.

Court. Used as in *court yard,* it refers to an unroofed, paved area next to the house (and garage in many of today's homes), giving shelter from wind and sun if properly solar-oriented.

Curtains. Hanging drapes of canvas, reed, or bamboo, designed to shut out the sun and wind, and offering only minor protection against rain. Curtains should be storable in winter. Must be replaced after a few seasons.

Deck. A floorlike surface, a deck differs basically from a patio in that it is created of wood above the ground, while a patio is built of concrete, stone, brick, or other such materials on the ground. A deck is advantageous where the ground slopes steeply, or where soil conditions present a problem for patio construction.

Mini-deck. Small deck providing minimum utility for sitting outdoors; as an entry or balcony it provides an area for intimate dining or sunbathing.

Engawa. A narrow catwalk used almost solely as a passageway or service platform for washing windows, and usually made of decking material.

Fence. Outdoor space divider that may be of wrought iron, wood, woven wire, split rail, railroad ties, or barbed wire. Varies greatly in height, color, design, and basic materials, according to its intended function. A fence is for screening undesirable views or areas, or for simple delineation of property.

Garden room. A separate, unroofed structure, set apart from the house, with walls on three sides and shade trees overhead. It is heavily outfitted with plantings in a variety of containers. It might be called a greenhouse without a roof.

Gazebo. A garden structure; the term is used here to denote a small square or octagonal shelter, floored and roofed, located in a secluded spot either with or without a view, but offering a retreat for one or two adults or several children. (*See* ARBOR, GARDEN ROOM, and PERGOLA).

Grid.   An open, overhead framing formed of uniformly spaced boards assembled perpendicular to each other in eggcrate fashion. Usually 1x6, 1x8, or 1x10 boards are used, depending on span to be covered. They are set on edge, and their depth determines amount of sun and shadow filtering downward onto deck or patio.

Ground cover.   Tanbark, gravel, colored stone, or sand, as most appropriate for activity area. Heavy plastic sheeting should be underlaid before this type of ground cover is put down, to prevent vegetation from growing through. Other forms of ground cover include ivy and creeping plantings, used to set off trees, shrubs, or to cover problem areas where grass will not grow.

Lanai.   Hawaiian term for veranda. A structural part of the house, open on at least one side, but covered on top by an extension of the roof. A view is essential.

Loggia.   A gallery or arcade open to the air on only one side but protected by three walls and roof of the house proper. It might be termed an elaborate lanai.

Overheads.   Similar to grid, but made of lightweight pipework, wood lath, or similar framing and designed specifically to support vines, reeds, or canvas which provides shade, whereas the grid itself is deep enough to accomplish this.

Patio.   As used here, *patio* refers to a surface supported by the ground formed of concrete, flagstone, slate, tile, or brick. We use the term to mean an open, outdoor living area, located either adjacent to a house or set as an island in the yard. It may be either flush with the ground line or raised perhaps 6 inches above it.

Pavilion.   A paved and roofed area adjacent to the house proper, open on three sides, and architecturally an integral part of the structure. Usually, columns are used to support the extended roof structure. It might be termed a formal lanai. (*See also* LOGGIA.)

Pathways.   Pathways are rustic, informal, and narrow but inviting trails through woods or gardens. They should be formed of grass, tamped dirt, soil-cement, tanbark, sand, or other natural materials, and serve only for light traffic. (*See* WALKWAYS.)

Pergola.   This garden structure is a somewhat more elaborate form of arbor, featuring heavy and ornate columns to support a more massive, open gridwork, over which vines or other foliage are trained. Its ground surface area is not necessarily paved. Any seating is usually built into the structure.

Portico.   A sheltering structure at the entry to a home, consisting of a roof in harmony with the architectural style of the house, and supported on columns or piers. Unfortunately, it is often too small to serve as an area for entertaining, but can be most inviting to welcome the guest.

Screening.   We use this term to denote both fencing of the man-made type, as well as the natural type—vines, shrubbery, and some types of trees (such as evergreens). Purpose of screening is to offer privacy, as a windbreak, or to shield undesirable areas such as compost heaps, garbage cans.

Terrace.   An open area, usually paved, adjacent to the house, where one or more sides of the area slope in abrupt descent. A series of such terraces is always dramatic and may be treated with decks and/or patios, as topography permits. In early Italy, artisans embedded marble chips in a thin grout of cement and water atop the roofs, often creating patterns. When hardened, this new surface was rubbed and polished. The result: terrazzo!

Trellis.   A garden structure, this ornamental framework of lattice is intended to support vertical vines and other climbing plants. It is customarily used on the sides of a gazebo or as a dramatic background for roses and other specimen plantings.

Veranda.   A large, open porch attached to the house, usually roofed over and often partially enclosed. It is also known in various parts of the country as a piazza or (depending on its size) a portico.

Walkways.   These differ basically from PATHWAYS in that they are wider and paved (brick, flagstone, railroad ties) to permit greater traffic.

Walls.   These differ from fences only in the type of materials from which they are made—fieldstone, brick, concrete block, and mortar. Walls are massive, require footings throughout their entire length. Remember, "fences float, walls sink."

Index